# UNIX AND LINUX
# SYSTEM ADMINISTRATION HANDBOOK

## MASTERING NETWORKING, SECURITY, CLOUD, PERFORMANCE, AND DEVOPS

# 4 BOOKS IN 1

### BOOK 1
UNIX AND LINUX SYSTEM ADMINISTRATION HANDBOOK: NETWORKING AND SECURITY ESSENTIALS

### BOOK 2
UNIX AND LINUX SYSTEM ADMINISTRATION HANDBOOK: CLOUD INTEGRATION AND INFRASTRUCTURE AS CODE

### BOOK 3
UNIX AND LINUX SYSTEM ADMINISTRATION HANDBOOK: PERFORMANCE TUNING AND SCALING

### BOOK 4
UNIX AND LINUX SYSTEM ADMINISTRATION HANDBOOK: DEVOPS AND CONTINUOUS INTEGRATION/CONTINUOUS DEPLOYMENT (CI/CD)

# ROB BOTWRIGHT

Published by Rob Botwright
Library of Congress Cataloging-in-Publication Data
ISBN 978-1-83938-588-9
Cover design by Rizzo

## Disclaimer

*The contents of this book are based on extensive research and the best available historical sources. However, the author and publisher make no claims, promises, or guarantees about the accuracy, completeness, or adequacy of the information contained herein. The information in this book is provided on an "as is" basis, and the author and publisher disclaim any and all liability for any errors, omissions, or inaccuracies in the information or for any actions taken in reliance on such information.*

*The opinions and views expressed in this book are those of the author and do not necessarily reflect the official policy or position of any organization or individual mentioned in this book. Any reference to specific people, places, or events is intended only to provide historical context and is not intended to defame or malign any group, individual, or entity.*

*The information in this book is intended for educational and entertainment purposes only. It is not intended to be a substitute for professional advice or judgment. Readers are encouraged to conduct their own research and to seek professional advice where appropriate.*

*Every effort has been made to obtain necessary permissions and acknowledgments for all images and other copyrighted material used in this book. Any errors or omissions in this regard are unintentional, and the author and publisher will correct them in future editions.*

## BOOK 1 - UNIX AND LINUX SYSTEM ADMINISTRATION HANDBOOK: NETWORKING AND SECURITY ESSENTIALS

## BOOK 2 - UNIX AND LINUX SYSTEM ADMINISTRATION HANDBOOK: CLOUD INTEGRATION AND INFRASTRUCTURE AS CODE

## BOOK 3 - UNIX AND LINUX SYSTEM ADMINISTRATION HANDBOOK: PERFORMANCE TUNING AND SCALING

## BOOK 4 - UNIX AND LINUX SYSTEM ADMINISTRATION HANDBOOK: DEVOPS AND CONTINUOUS INTEGRATION/CONTINUOUS DEPLOYMENT (CI/CD)

# Introduction

In the ever-evolving landscape of information technology, the role of system administrators is more critical than ever before. System administrators are the unsung heroes behind the scenes, ensuring that the intricate machinery of UNIX and Linux systems operates seamlessly and securely. As technology advances at an unprecedented pace, so too must the knowledge and skills of those tasked with its management.

Enter the "UNIX and Linux System Administration Handbook: Mastering Networking, Security, Cloud, Performance, and DevOps" bundle. This comprehensive collection of books is designed to equip both aspiring and seasoned system administrators with the knowledge, techniques, and best practices needed to excel in their roles.

Within this bundle, we have assembled a treasure trove of expertise spanning a multitude of crucial domains. Each book is a standalone guide, meticulously crafted to provide a deep dive into a specific aspect of system administration. Together, they create a unified and unparalleled resource that addresses the holistic spectrum of responsibilities and challenges faced by today's system administrators.

Book 1, "UNIX and Linux System Administration Handbook: Networking and Security Essentials," serves as your gateway into the world of system administration. It explores the fundamental concepts of networking and security, laying a solid foundation upon which the rest of your knowledge will be built.

Book 2, "UNIX and Linux System Administration Handbook: Cloud Integration and Infrastructure as Code," propels you into the future of IT. It demystifies the complexities of cloud computing and introduces you to the paradigm-shifting concept of Infrastructure as Code (IaC).

Book 3, "UNIX and Linux System Administration Handbook: Performance Tuning and Scaling," empowers you to unlock the full potential of your systems. Dive deep into the art and science of performance optimization, ensuring your systems run at peak efficiency.

Book 4, "UNIX and Linux System Administration Handbook: DevOps and Continuous Integration/Continuous Deployment (CI/CD)," invites you to embrace the transformative world of DevOps. Learn how to automate, collaborate, and streamline your development processes.

Throughout this bundle, you'll find not just technical guidance but also real-world insights and practical advice from experienced professionals who have navigated the complexities of system administration. Whether you're seeking to enhance your skills, troubleshoot challenging issues, or prepare for the future of IT, this bundle is your indispensable companion.

So, whether you're a seasoned administrator looking to sharpen your expertise or a newcomer eager to embark on a fulfilling journey, welcome to the "UNIX and Linux System Administration Handbook: Mastering Networking, Security, Cloud, Performance, and DevOps" bundle. Let's embark on this educational odyssey together, where knowledge becomes power, and mastery becomes second nature.

**BOOK 1**
***UNIX AND LINUX SYSTEM ADMINISTRATION HANDBOOK***
***NETWORKING AND SECURITY ESSENTIALS***

***ROB BOTWRIGHT***

*In the world of technology and operating systems, the histories of UNIX and Linux stand as pivotal narratives, representing the evolution of computing since the mid-20th century. UNIX, often hailed as the mother of modern operating systems, traces its origins back to the late 1960s when Ken Thompson, Dennis Ritchie, and their colleagues at AT&T's Bell Labs developed the first version, later known as "First Edition UNIX." Over the years, UNIX went through several iterations and became a standard in academia and industry, known for its flexibility and powerful command-line interface. The 1970s brought the development of C, a programming language that became instrumental in UNIX's growth and portability, allowing it to be adapted to different hardware platforms. UNIX's widespread adoption continued into the 1980s, with various commercial versions such as System III, System V, and BSD (Berkeley Software Distribution) UNIX, each offering unique features and capabilities.*

*Simultaneously, the GNU project, initiated by Richard Stallman in the 1980s, aimed to create a free and open-source UNIX-like operating system. Stallman's vision gave birth to the Free Software Foundation (FSF) and the GNU General Public License (GPL), which encouraged collaboration and the sharing of source code. This philosophy laid the foundation for the open-source movement and eventually played a crucial role in the development of Linux. In the early 1990s, Linus Torvalds, a Finnish computer science student, created the Linux kernel, which combined with the GNU utilities, formed a complete, free, and open-source UNIX-like operating system. This union marked the birth of Linux and set the stage for its rapid growth and popularity.*

*The 1990s saw the emergence of various Linux distributions, each offering its unique blend of software packages and configurations. Debian, Red Hat, Slackware, and SuSE were among the pioneering distributions, catering to different user needs and preferences. Linux's scalability, robustness, and cost-effectiveness made it an attractive choice for diverse applications, ranging from servers to embedded systems and personal computers. Its collaborative development model allowed a global community of developers to contribute to its codebase continually, resulting in constant improvement and innovation.*

*Throughout the 2000s and beyond, Linux's influence extended beyond traditional computing platforms. It became the dominant operating system for servers, powering a significant portion of the internet's infrastructure. Linux-based Android OS revolutionized the smartphone industry, while embedded Linux found its way into countless devices, from smart TVs to automotive systems. Furthermore, the rise of containerization technologies like Docker and Kubernetes further solidified Linux's importance in the realm of modern cloud computing and DevOps.*

*The journey of UNIX and Linux also includes the concept of shells, which are command-line interfaces that enable users to interact with the operating system. The Bourne shell, created by Stephen Bourne in the 1970s, was the original UNIX shell and laid the groundwork for subsequent shells like the C shell (csh) and the Korn shell (ksh). However, one shell that gained immense popularity* was the Bourne-Again Shell (bash), created by Brian Fox in the late 1980s. Bash became the default shell for Linux distributions and is still widely used today due to its extensive features and scripting capabilities.

Security has always been a critical aspect of UNIX and Linux. The "Principle of Least Privilege" was a foundational concept in UNIX, emphasizing the need to restrict user privileges to minimize potential security risks. Features like user and group management, file permissions, and access control lists (ACLs) allowed administrators to implement strong security practices. Additionally, tools such as SELinux (Security-Enhanced Linux) and AppArmor further enhanced security by providing mandatory access controls and confinement for applications.

As Linux and open-source software gained prominence, cybersecurity experts worldwide scrutinized the codebase, leading to rapid vulnerability discovery and patching. The community's responsiveness and collaboration helped create a robust security ecosystem, making Linux a secure choice for critical applications and sensitive data. However, security is an ongoing concern, and administrators must remain vigilant by applying updates and implementing best practices to mitigate potential risks.

The synergy between UNIX and Linux extended into the corporate world, where businesses recognized the value of open-source solutions. Companies like IBM, Red Hat, and SUSE played pivotal roles in providing enterprise-grade Linux distributions and support. The Linux ecosystem flourished with a vibrant ecosystem of software vendors, offering solutions for everything from database management to application development. As a result,

Linux became a top choice for data centers, cloud computing, and mission-critical applications across industries.

In the realm of desktop computing, Linux offered an alternative to proprietary operating systems like Microsoft Windows and macOS. Distributions like Ubuntu, Fedora, and Linux Mint aimed to provide user-friendly, intuitive desktop environments, making Linux accessible to a broader audience. The Linux community worked tirelessly to improve hardware compatibility, develop robust office productivity suites, and offer diverse software options, making Linux a viable choice for personal computing.

The evolution of UNIX and Linux is an ongoing narrative, continually adapting to the ever-changing landscape of technology. From servers and embedded systems to cloud computing and personal devices, UNIX and Linux continue to shape the digital world. Their stories reflect the power of collaboration, innovation, and the enduring commitment to free and open-source principles. As we look to the future, the legacy of UNIX and Linux remains an inspiration for generations of technologists and open-source enthusiasts, serving as a testament to the enduring impact of these operating systems on our digital lives.

In the intricate realm of modern computing, the role of a system administrator emerges as a linchpin in the smooth functioning of information technology infrastructures. These unsung heroes work tirelessly behind the scenes, managing servers, networks, and devices to ensure that organizations can harness the full potential of technology for their operations. A system administrator is akin to a digital conductor, orchestrating a symphony of software, hardware, and networks to create a harmonious computing environment. Their responsibilities span a wide spectrum, from setting up and configuring servers to troubleshooting issues, implementing security measures, and optimizing performance. The role is not confined to a single domain but encompasses a multitude of tasks that vary depending on the organization's size, industry, and specific needs. One of the fundamental tasks of a system administrator is server management, which includes provisioning, maintaining, and monitoring servers to ensure they are always available and performing optimally. This entails selecting the appropriate hardware, installing and configuring the operating system, and setting up essential software components. Additionally, system administrators are tasked with managing server resources efficiently, such as allocating CPU, memory, and storage as needed for various applications and services. Security is another critical aspect of the role, as system administrators play a pivotal role in safeguarding an organization's digital assets. They must implement and maintain security measures like firewalls, intrusion detection systems, and access controls to protect against cyber threats. This involves staying up-to-date with the latest security vulnerabilities and patches to promptly address potential weaknesses. Furthermore, system administrators are responsible for creating and enforcing security policies and practices within the organization. Network administration is another vital component of the role, encompassing tasks like designing and maintaining network architectures, managing switches and routers, and ensuring network connectivity and reliability. This involves configuring network devices, monitoring traffic, and troubleshooting connectivity issues to keep data flowing seamlessly. In today's interconnected world, the role of a system administrator extends beyond the physical boundaries of an organization's infrastructure. Cloud computing has introduced a new dimension to their responsibilities, as they must navigate cloud platforms and services to optimize resources and ensure data integrity and availability. The rise of virtualization technology has also transformed the landscape, allowing administrators to create and manage virtual machines efficiently. System administrators often use tools like VMware, Hyper-V, and KVM to provision and manage virtual environments, reducing hardware costs and enhancing flexibility. Automation plays a pivotal role in modern system administration, enabling administrators to streamline repetitive tasks and reduce manual intervention. Tools like Ansible, Puppet, and Chef allow them to automate configuration management, software deployment, and system provisioning, saving time and reducing the risk of human errors. Monitoring and performance optimization are constant tasks for system administrators. They employ monitoring tools to keep a vigilant eye on system health, identifying bottlenecks, and addressing issues proactively. By analyzing performance data and making adjustments, they ensure that systems operate at peak efficiency. Backup and disaster recovery planning is a crucial part of the role, involving the creation and maintenance of data backup strategies and disaster recovery plans. System administrators implement backup solutions, regularly test recovery procedures, and ensure data integrity to minimize downtime in case of unexpected events. Collaboration and communication skills are essential for system administrators, as they often work closely with other IT professionals, department heads, and end-users. They need to explain technical issues in a comprehensible manner, collaborate with cross-functional teams, and understand the unique technology needs of different departments within an organization. Documentation is another crucial aspect of the role, as system administrators must maintain detailed records of configurations, changes, and incident reports. Well-organized documentation ensures that procedures are repeatable, and knowledge can be transferred seamlessly in the event of personnel changes. In the context of cybersecurity, system administrators play a pivotal role in incident response and forensics. They must be prepared to investigate security breaches, analyze compromised systems, and take corrective actions to mitigate risks and prevent future incidents. Education and staying updated with the latest industry trends and technologies are perpetual requirements for system administrators. The IT landscape evolves rapidly, and keeping pace with new developments is essential to remain effective in the role. Certifications like CompTIA A+, Microsoft Certified System Administrator (MCSA), or Certified Information Systems Security Professional (CISSP) can help validate skills and knowledge. Soft skills are equally critical for success in the role, as system administrators need to communicate effectively, work well under pressure, and adapt to changing circumstances. Problem-solving and critical thinking abilities are essential for diagnosing complex issues and devising innovative solutions. The role of a system administrator is not without its challenges, from dealing with unexpected system failures to addressing the *ever-present threat of cyberattacks. However, it is also a role that offers immense satisfaction, as system administrators are the unsung heroes behind the scenes, ensuring that technology serves as an enabler rather than an obstacle. Their expertise and dedication are instrumental in the smooth operation of businesses, government agencies, educational institutions, and countless other organizations worldwide. In summary, the role of a system administrator is multifaceted, encompassing server management, security, networking, virtualization, automation, monitoring, and more. System administrators are the custodians of an organization's technology infrastructure, ensuring its reliability, security, and performance. They adapt to the evolving IT landscape, embracing new technologies and methodologies to fulfill their mission of enabling organizations to thrive in the digital age.*

*In the vast landscape of modern communication and information technology, various types of networks have emerged, each designed to serve specific purposes and address unique requirements. One of the most common types of networks is the Local Area Network (LAN), which is typically confined to a relatively small geographic area, such as a home, office, or campus. LANs enable devices like computers, printers, and servers to share resources and communicate with one another efficiently. Ethernet and Wi-Fi are commonly used technologies for implementing LANs, providing wired and wireless connectivity options, respectively. As organizations grow and their networking needs expand, they often turn to Wide Area Networks (WANs) to connect geographically dispersed locations. WANs bridge the gap between distant LANs, enabling seamless communication between sites separated by considerable distances. The internet itself can be considered the largest and most extensive WAN, connecting individuals, businesses, and institutions across the globe. WAN technologies include leased lines, Frame Relay, and MPLS (Multi-Protocol Label Switching), which provide reliable and high-speed connections over long distances. For even broader connectivity, there are Metropolitan Area Networks (MANs), which cover a larger geographic area than LANs but are smaller than WANs, often encompassing an entire city. MANs are employed in scenarios where organizations need to connect multiple locations within a metropolitan area, such as government agencies or educational institutions. A key feature of*

MANs is their ability to provide high-speed connections, making them suitable for data-intensive applications. As technology advances, so do the needs of various industries, and this has given rise to specialized networks tailored to specific requirements. One notable example is Storage Area Networks (SANs), designed to provide high-speed access to shared storage resources, such as disk arrays and tape libraries. SANs are commonly used in data centers, enabling efficient data storage and retrieval for mission-critical applications. Another specialized network type is the Campus Area Network (CAN), which serves to connect multiple LANs within a limited geographic area, such as a university campus or corporate headquarters. CANs provide high-speed connectivity to support large-scale data transfer and communication among different departments or units within the same organization. The advent of mobile devices and the demand for ubiquitous connectivity have given rise to wireless networks, including Wireless Local Area Networks (WLANs) and Cellular Networks. WLANs use Wi-Fi technology to provide wireless connectivity within a confined area, allowing users to access the internet and network resources without the need for physical cables. Cellular networks, on the other hand, use a network of cell towers to provide mobile phone and data services, enabling users to stay connected while on the move. A less common but highly specialized network is the Industrial Control System (ICS) network, which is crucial for managing and controlling industrial processes and critical infrastructure. ICS networks are commonly found in manufacturing plants, power plants, and utilities, facilitating the monitoring and operation of complex machinery and systems. To ensure the integrity *and security of ICS networks, they are often isolated from conventional IT networks to prevent unauthorized access or cyberattacks. The emergence of the Internet of Things (IoT) has introduced a new dimension to networking, with millions of interconnected devices and sensors that collect and exchange data over the internet. IoT networks are characterized by their vast scale and diversity, as they can include anything from smart home devices to industrial sensors and autonomous vehicles. These networks require robust security measures to protect sensitive data and ensure the reliability of connected devices. In the realm of telecommunications, there are Public Switched Telephone Networks (PSTNs), which have been the backbone of voice communication for decades. PSTNs use circuit-switching technology to establish and maintain voice connections between callers, making them suitable for traditional telephone services. In contrast, Voice over Internet Protocol (VoIP) networks use packet-switching technology to transmit voice calls over the internet, offering cost-effective and feature-rich communication solutions. Virtual Private Networks (VPNs) are a type of network that provides secure and encrypted communication over public networks like the internet. VPNs are commonly used by individuals and organizations to ensure data privacy and protect sensitive information from eavesdropping and cyber threats. In the world of finance and stock trading, Financial Information Exchange (FIX) networks facilitate the rapid and secure exchange of financial data and trade orders between financial institutions and exchanges. FIX networks are known for their low latency and high reliability, crucial factors in the fast-paced world of financial trading. In healthcare, there are Health*

*Information Exchange (HIE) networks that enable the sharing of medical information among healthcare providers, improving patient care coordination and reducing medical errors. These networks play a pivotal role in modern healthcare delivery by ensuring that patient data is accessible to authorized healthcare professionals when needed. An emerging and highly innovative network type is the Software-Defined Network (SDN), which leverages software to dynamically manage and optimize network resources. SDNs provide greater flexibility and control over network traffic, making them ideal for cloud computing environments and data center networking. Mesh networks are a decentralized type of network in which each node connects directly to multiple other nodes, forming a resilient and self-healing network. Mesh networks are often used in scenarios where traditional network infrastructure is impractical, such as disaster recovery or remote rural areas. Peer-to-Peer (P2P) networks are designed for distributed file sharing and communication, allowing users to share resources directly with one another without relying on centralized servers. P2P networks have gained popularity for file sharing, video conferencing, and decentralized applications. These various types of networks serve as the backbone of our interconnected world, supporting a multitude of applications and industries. Their diversity reflects the evolving needs and technological advancements that drive the continuous development of network infrastructure. In an era where connectivity and data exchange are paramount, understanding these network types and their unique characteristics is crucial for individuals, businesses, and organizations seeking to harness the power of modern*

*networking                                    technologies.*
*In the intricate realm of computer networking, the concept of network topologies plays a fundamental and pivotal role, defining the physical and logical layout of how devices and nodes are interconnected. These topologies serve as the blueprints for communication, determining how data travels between devices, and influencing factors like reliability, scalability, and fault tolerance. One of the most basic and commonly encountered network topologies is the Bus Topology, where all devices are connected to a single central cable or bus. In a bus topology, devices are attached to the main cable through connectors or taps, and data is transmitted in both directions along the bus. While simple and cost-effective, bus topologies can suffer from performance issues if too many devices are connected or if there is a break in the main cable, causing network disruption. In contrast, the Star Topology centers around a central hub or switch, with each device connected directly to this central point. Data is transmitted through the hub, allowing for efficient communication between devices. Star topologies are easy to set up and manage, and if one device fails, it doesn't necessarily disrupt the entire network. However, the central hub represents a single point of failure, and the scalability of the network can be limited by the hub's capacity. For scenarios where redundancy and fault tolerance are paramount, the Ring Topology is employed, where devices are connected in a closed loop. Data travels in a unidirectional or bidirectional manner around the ring until it reaches its destination. Ring topologies are highly fault-tolerant, as data can still flow in the opposite direction if a break in the ring occurs. However, adding or*

removing devices can be complex, as it requires the network to be temporarily disrupted. Mesh Topologies take redundancy to the extreme, with each device directly connected to every other device in the network. Full mesh topologies offer unparalleled fault tolerance, as there are multiple paths for data to travel. These topologies are often used in critical applications where network reliability is of utmost importance, such as in financial institutions and data centers. The downside is that the cabling and configuration complexity can be prohibitive, especially as the network scales. Hybrid Topologies combine elements of different topologies to balance strengths and weaknesses. For instance, a common hybrid approach is to use a star topology for individual departments within an organization and then connect these star networks with a bus or ring topology at a higher level. This combines the ease of management of star topologies with the fault tolerance of ring or bus topologies. Logical topologies, on the other hand, refer to how data is transmitted and routed in a network, irrespective of its physical layout. Ethernet networks often employ logical topologies such as Ethernet bus or Ethernet star, regardless of the physical cabling arrangement. Point-to-Point (P2P) and Point-to-Multipoint (P2MP) are logical topologies used in telecommunications to describe the flow of data between devices. In a P2P configuration, data travels directly between two endpoints, while in a P2MP configuration, data is broadcast from one point to multiple receiving points. Understanding network topologies is essential for network administrators and engineers, as it dictates how data flows, how devices are connected, and how potential points of failure can be mitigated. Selecting the *appropriate topology depends on factors like the organization's requirements, the type of data being transmitted, scalability needs, and budget constraints. The evolution of network technologies has introduced new possibilities and variations of traditional topologies. For instance, the advent of wireless technology has given rise to the Wireless Mesh Topology, where wireless nodes form an interconnected mesh network, providing flexibility and adaptability. Another modern development is the Virtual LAN (VLAN), a logical segmentation of a physical network into multiple virtual networks. VLANs enable network administrators to control broadcast domains, enhance security, and optimize network traffic. Modern data centers often employ a Clos Network Topology, also known as a fat-tree topology, which offers high bandwidth and fault tolerance for large-scale server environments. In Clos topologies, switches are interconnected in multiple layers, creating multiple paths for data and redundancy. These topologies are well-suited for the high-performance demands of data center applications. When it comes to wide area networks (WANs), Multiprotocol Label Switching (MPLS) has gained popularity as a logical topology for efficient data routing and forwarding. MPLS networks use labels to determine the most efficient path for data transmission, allowing for faster and more reliable wide-area communication. Peer-to-peer (P2P) networks have evolved beyond simple file sharing to encompass distributed technologies like blockchain. Blockchain networks utilize a decentralized ledger to record transactions across a network of nodes. This distributed ledger technology has found applications in cryptocurrencies, supply chain management, and more. As technology continues to advance, network topologies will evolve to meet the ever-growing demands of our interconnected world. Emerging technologies like the Internet of Things (IoT), edge computing, and 5G connectivity will reshape how networks are designed and deployed. Understanding and adapting to these changes will remain a vital skill for network professionals and organizations seeking to harness the full potential of their networks in an increasingly digital landscape.*

*In the realm of networking and internet communication, the TCP/IP protocol suite stands as a cornerstone, underpinning the vast interconnected web of devices, services, and data that defines the digital age. This suite of protocols provides the essential framework for transmitting and receiving data across networks, facilitating the seamless flow of information across the internet and within private networks. At its core, TCP/IP comprises two primary protocols: the Transmission Control Protocol (TCP) and the Internet Protocol (IP). TCP is responsible for establishing and maintaining reliable connections between devices, ensuring that data arrives intact and in the correct order. IP, on the other hand, handles the addressing and routing of data packets, determining how data reaches its intended destination across networks. Together, TCP and IP work harmoniously to enable robust and efficient communication across the internet and local networks. The story of TCP/IP dates back to the early days of computer networking when the U.S. Department of Defense initiated the ARPANET project in the late 1960s. The need for a standardized, robust, and adaptable communication protocol became apparent as researchers and engineers connected various computer systems and networks. In response, the TCP/IP protocol suite emerged as a solution, with the initial development efforts led by Vinton Cerf and Bob Kahn in the 1970s. Their work resulted in the creation of the Internet Protocol (IP) and the Transmission Control Protocol (TCP), which were documented in a series of seminal publications known as*

*RFCs (Request for Comments). The TCP/IP protocols were designed to be platform-agnostic, allowing different types of computer systems and networks to communicate seamlessly. This foundational principle, along with its open and extensible architecture, contributed to the rapid adoption of TCP/IP as the de facto standard for internet communication. One of the defining features of TCP is its reliable data transfer mechanism, achieved through a combination of acknowledgment and retransmission. When data is sent over a TCP connection, the sender waits for acknowledgment from the receiver to confirm the successful receipt of each data segment. If an acknowledgment is not received within a specified time frame, the sender retransmits the data segment to ensure its delivery. This reliability mechanism ensures that data sent over the internet arrives intact and in the correct order, even in the presence of network congestion or errors. In contrast, the Internet Protocol (IP) focuses on addressing and routing data packets across networks, with each device assigned a unique IP address. These addresses serve as virtual destinations for data packets, allowing routers and switches to determine how to forward them to their intended recipients. IPv4 (Internet Protocol version 4) was the original version of IP and used a 32-bit address format, which allowed for approximately 4.3 billion unique addresses. While IPv4 served the internet well for many years, the explosive growth of internet-connected devices in the late 20th and early 21st centuries exhausted the available address space. In response, IPv6 (Internet Protocol version 6) was introduced, featuring a 128-bit address format capable of accommodating an astronomical number of unique addresses. IPv6 adoption* has been steadily increasing to address the growing demands of the internet and ensure its continued growth. Beyond TCP and IP, the TCP/IP protocol suite encompasses a range of auxiliary protocols and services, each with its specific role and functionality. For instance, the Internet Control Message Protocol (ICMP) is responsible for error reporting and diagnostics, often used for tools like ping and traceroute. The User Datagram Protocol (UDP) offers a lightweight, connectionless transport protocol suitable for applications where low overhead and speed are prioritized over reliability. Additional protocols like the Simple Network Management Protocol (SNMP) facilitate network management and monitoring, while the Domain Name System (DNS) translates human-readable domain names into IP addresses. The evolution of the TCP/IP protocol suite has been marked by ongoing enhancements and adaptations to meet the changing needs of the internet and networking environments. Quality of Service (QoS) mechanisms, such as Differentiated Services (DiffServ) and Resource Reservation Protocol (RSVP), have been introduced to manage and prioritize network traffic. Security considerations have led to the development of protocols like the Internet Security Protocol (IPsec) to encrypt and authenticate data communications. Furthermore, advancements like Multiprotocol Label Switching (MPLS) have improved the efficiency and scalability of IP-based networks. As the internet continues to expand and diversify, the role of the TCP/IP protocol suite remains pivotal in enabling global connectivity and information exchange. The open nature of TCP/IP, its interoperability across diverse platforms, and its resilience in the face of network challenges have solidified its position as the backbone of modern communication. From web browsing and email to cloud computing and IoT (Internet of Things) applications, TCP/IP serves as the invisible hand that guides data through the intricate web of interconnected devices and networks. The ubiquity and adaptability of TCP/IP ensure its enduring relevance in an ever-evolving digital landscape, where innovation and connectivity drive the future of communication and information exchange.

In the intricate tapestry of computer networks, a multitude of network protocols weave together the threads of communication, facilitating the exchange of data, information, and resources. These protocols serve as the rules and conventions that govern how devices on a network communicate and collaborate, ensuring that data can be transmitted, received, and understood by all parties involved. One of the most fundamental and ubiquitous network protocols is the Internet Protocol (IP), a cornerstone of the TCP/IP protocol suite that underpins the internet and most modern networks. IP is responsible for addressing and routing data packets, allowing them to traverse the complex web of interconnected devices and networks that comprise the global internet. IPv4, the most widely used version of IP, employs a 32-bit address format to uniquely identify devices on the network, while IPv6, its successor, uses a 128-bit address format to accommodate the ever-expanding landscape of internet-connected devices. Transmission Control Protocol (TCP), another key component of the TCP/IP suite, provides reliable, connection-oriented communication between devices by ensuring that data is delivered in the correct order and without errors. TCP employs mechanisms like acknowledgment and retransmission to guarantee the delivery of data, making it an essential protocol for applications that require data integrity and consistency, such as web browsing and email. User Datagram Protocol (UDP), also part of the TCP/IP suite, offers a lightweight, connectionless transport protocol suitable for applications where speed and low overhead are prioritized over reliability. UDP is commonly used for real-time communication, including voice and video streaming, online gaming, and networked applications where a small amount of data loss is acceptable. Another critical network protocol is the Internet Control Message Protocol (ICMP), which is primarily used for error reporting and diagnostics. ICMP enables devices to communicate important network-related information, such as unreachable destinations, network congestion, or time exceeded for packet delivery. ICMP messages are integral to tools like ping and traceroute, which network administrators rely on to troubleshoot connectivity issues. The Hypertext Transfer Protocol (HTTP) and its secure counterpart, HTTPS, are essential application layer protocols that govern how web browsers and web servers communicate. HTTP defines the rules for requesting and delivering web pages and resources, enabling users to access websites and web-based applications. HTTPS adds a layer of security by encrypting data exchanged between the client (browser) and server, safeguarding sensitive information such as login credentials and financial transactions. File Transfer Protocol (FTP) is a protocol designed for transferring files between a client and a server on a network. FTP facilitates the uploading and downloading of files and directories, making it a standard protocol for managing files and data on remote servers. Another file transfer protocol, the Trivial File Transfer Protocol (TFTP), simplifies file transfers by providing a minimalistic and connectionless approach, making it suitable for tasks like updating firmware on network devices. The Simple Mail Transfer Protocol (SMTP) is dedicated to the transmission of email messages, allowing email clients to send messages to email servers for delivery. SMTP ensures that emails are routed correctly and delivered to the recipient's mailbox, serving as the backbone of electronic mail communication. Post Office Protocol version 3 (POP3) and Internet Message Access Protocol (IMAP) are protocols used by email clients to retrieve messages from email servers. POP3 downloads emails to the client's device, typically removing them from the server, while IMAP synchronizes emails across multiple devices, enabling users to access their messages from various clients while retaining them on the server. The Domain Name System (DNS) is a crucial network protocol that translates human-readable domain names, such as www.example.com, into IP addresses, facilitating the routing of internet traffic. DNS ensures that users can access websites and services using easily memorable domain names rather than numeric IP addresses. Dynamic Host Configuration Protocol (DHCP) automates the assignment of IP addresses and network configuration parameters to devices on a network. DHCP simplifies network management by eliminating the need for manual IP address assignment, enabling devices to join the network seamlessly. Network Time Protocol (NTP) is essential for synchronizing the clocks of devices on a network, ensuring that they maintain accurate time and coordinate activities effectively. NTP is crucial for *applications and systems that rely on precise timing, such as financial transactions and network security protocols. Secure Shell (SSH) is a cryptographic network protocol used for secure remote access to devices and servers over an unsecured network. SSH encrypts data transmitted between the client and server, protecting sensitive information and providing secure remote administration and file transfer capabilities. The Border Gateway Protocol (BGP) is the protocol that governs the routing of data between different autonomous systems (ASes) on the internet. BGP is instrumental in determining the most efficient path for data to traverse the global internet, ensuring efficient routing and fault tolerance. Simple Network Management Protocol (SNMP) is a network management protocol used for monitoring and managing network devices, including routers, switches, and servers. SNMP allows administrators to collect information about device performance, monitor network health, and configure devices remotely. While these are some of the most commonly encountered network protocols, the world of networking is vast and continually evolving. Emerging technologies, such as the Internet of Things (IoT), bring new protocols and challenges as devices become more interconnected and require specialized communication standards. Understanding these network protocols and their roles in the broader landscape of networking is essential for network administrators, engineers, and anyone navigating the intricacies of modern computer networks. These protocols form the foundation of the digital world, enabling the seamless flow of data and information that underpins our interconnected lives.*

*In the realm of network security, firewalls stand as sentinels, guarding the digital fortresses of organizations and individuals against the relentless tide of cyber threats. These critical security devices act as barriers between trusted internal networks and the uncharted waters of the internet, regulating the flow of traffic and determining which data packets are permitted entry. Firewalls come in various forms and types, each designed to fulfill specific security needs and objectives, making them integral components of modern network defense strategies. One of the most common types of firewalls is the network-based firewall, often deployed at the perimeter of a network to safeguard it from external threats. Network-based firewalls analyze incoming and outgoing network traffic, enforcing predefined security rules and policies to permit or deny access to network resources. These firewalls are equipped with features such as stateful inspection, intrusion detection, and intrusion prevention, offering comprehensive protection against a wide range of cyberattacks. Packet-filtering firewalls, a subset of network-based firewalls, examine individual packets of data as they traverse the network. They inspect packet headers and make decisions based on predefined rules, such as allowing or blocking traffic based on source and destination IP addresses, port numbers, and protocols. Packet-filtering firewalls are efficient and suitable for basic security needs but may lack the granularity and advanced features of other firewall types. Proxy firewalls, also known as application-level gateways (ALGs), operate at the application layer of the OSI model, making them highly effective at filtering and controlling specific applications and services. These firewalls act as intermediaries between clients and servers, inspecting and filtering traffic at the application level. Proxy firewalls can provide deep packet inspection, content filtering, and enhanced security for applications like web browsing and email. Stateful inspection firewalls, often referred to as dynamic packet filtering firewalls, maintain a stateful table of active connections. They monitor the state and context of network sessions, allowing them to make more informed decisions about whether to permit or block traffic. Stateful inspection firewalls combine the benefits of packet filtering and application layer inspection, offering robust security with improved performance. Next-generation firewalls (NGFWs) represent a more advanced breed of network-based firewalls, combining traditional firewall capabilities with deep packet inspection, intrusion prevention, antivirus, and application awareness. NGFWs are designed to combat sophisticated threats and offer granular control over applications and users. While network-based firewalls primarily focus on protecting network perimeters, host-based firewalls operate on individual devices, such as servers and workstations. These firewalls provide an additional layer of defense by controlling inbound and outbound traffic at the device level. Host-based firewalls are particularly valuable for protecting endpoints against malware and unauthorized access. Firewalls can also be categorized based on their deployment mode, with some designed to be hardware appliances, while others are implemented as software solutions. Hardware firewalls are standalone devices* dedicated to the task of network security. They are often deployed at the network perimeter and offer robust protection for entire networks. Hardware firewalls come in various form factors, including dedicated appliances and integrated devices like routers and switches. Software firewalls, on the other hand, are installed on individual computers or servers, providing protection at the device level. These firewalls are commonly used to protect endpoints and can be customized to suit specific security requirements. Another category of firewalls includes cloud-based or virtual firewalls, which are designed for cloud-native and virtualized environments. These firewalls offer scalable and flexible security solutions for cloud-based applications and virtual machines. Cloud-based firewalls are often managed through a centralized cloud console, making them ideal for distributed and dynamic network architectures. Firewalls can also be classified based on the techniques they employ for filtering and decision-making. Stateless firewalls, as the name suggests, do not maintain any knowledge of the state or context of network connections. They examine each packet in isolation and make filtering decisions based solely on predefined rules. Stateless firewalls are fast and lightweight but may lack the context-awareness of stateful firewalls. Stateful firewalls, on the other hand, maintain a state table that tracks the state of active network connections. They keep track of the state of each connection, allowing them to make more informed decisions about whether to permit or block traffic. This stateful inspection enables stateful firewalls to provide enhanced security and improved performance. Intrusion Detection System (IDS) firewalls combine firewall *capabilities with intrusion detection functionality. They not only filter and control network traffic but also analyze it for signs of suspicious or malicious activity. IDS firewalls can detect and alert administrators to potential security breaches, making them valuable tools for proactive threat detection. Unified Threat Management (UTM) firewalls go a step further by integrating multiple security features into a single device. UTM firewalls typically include firewalling, intrusion detection and prevention, antivirus, content filtering, and more. These all-in-one solutions provide comprehensive protection against a wide range of threats. Firewalls play a pivotal role in modern cybersecurity, forming the first line of defense against an ever-evolving landscape of cyber threats. Their versatility and adaptability make them indispensable tools for safeguarding networks, devices, and data. Whether deployed at the network perimeter, on individual devices, or in the cloud, firewalls remain essential components of a robust security posture, helping organizations navigate the digital age with confidence and resilience. In the realm of network security, firewall rules and policies serve as the bedrock upon which effective defenses are built, determining what is allowed and what is denied within a network. These rules act as gatekeepers, regulating the flow of data packets and traffic, ensuring that only authorized communications traverse the digital boundaries. Firewall rules, often referred to as access control rules or filtering rules, are the fundamental building blocks of firewall policies. These rules define specific conditions that packets must meet to be allowed or denied entry into a network. A typical firewall rule consists of criteria such as source and destination IP addresses, source and destination port numbers, and the protocol used. Firewall rules can be granular, allowing for fine-tuned control over network traffic, or they can be broad, permitting or blocking entire categories of traffic. One of the key decisions in creating firewall rules is determining whether to allow or deny traffic based on the specified criteria. Allow rules permit traffic that meets the criteria, while deny rules block traffic that matches the specified conditions. Effective firewall rule management involves striking a balance between allowing the necessary traffic for legitimate network operations and blocking potentially harmful or unauthorized traffic. Implicit deny rules, a fundamental concept in firewall policies, dictate that if a packet does not match any of the explicitly defined allow rules, it is implicitly denied by default. This ensures that, by default, only traffic explicitly permitted by the defined rules is allowed to traverse the firewall. The order in which firewall rules are evaluated is critical, as it can impact the effectiveness of the policy. Rules are typically processed in a sequential manner, and the first rule that matches a packet's criteria determines whether the packet is allowed or denied. The sequence of rules in a firewall policy can significantly influence how traffic is filtered and should be carefully considered to ensure the desired level of security. Firewall policies often employ a top-down approach, with rules ordered from most specific to least specific. This arrangement ensures that rules with narrow criteria take precedence over broader rules, reducing the risk of unintended consequences. One common practice is to begin with a set of broad deny rules that block traffic from known malicious IP addresses or entire countries. Following these, allow rules are defined for specific trusted sources, services, or applications that need to communicate with the network. Careful rule organization and documentation are essential for maintaining a clear and effective firewall policy. Network administrators must continuously review and update firewall rules to adapt to changing network requirements and emerging threats. Firewall policies can become complex as the network evolves, with rules covering various services, protocols, and user groups. To manage this complexity, some organizations adopt a principle known as the principle of least privilege (PoLP). PoLP dictates that only the minimum level of access necessary for a user or system to perform its functions should be granted. Applying this principle to firewall rules helps limit potential attack vectors and reduces the risk of unauthorized access. Another consideration in firewall rule management is the use of rule sets or rule groups. Rule sets group related rules together, making it easier to manage and understand complex policies. For example, all rules related to web traffic may be grouped into a "Web Services" rule set, while email-related rules form an "Email Services" rule set. This logical organization enhances policy clarity and simplifies rule updates. Firewall rules can also be applied to specific zones or network segments. Segmenting a network into zones allows for different security policies to be applied to each segment, providing granular control over traffic. For instance, a DMZ (Demilitarized Zone) may have distinct firewall rules compared to an internal network segment. As networks evolve, the need for advanced firewall features becomes apparent. Modern firewalls often incorporate deep packet inspection (DPI), intrusion detection and prevention (IDP), and application layer filtering into their rule sets. These advanced capabilities enable firewalls to detect and block threats that traditional rule-based filtering may miss. Application-aware firewalls, for example, can inspect the content of data packets to identify and control specific applications or services, ensuring that only authorized applications are allowed. Intrusion detection and prevention systems (IDPS) go beyond simple rule-based filtering, using advanced techniques to detect and block potentially malicious activity based on known attack patterns and behaviors. Effective firewall rule management extends beyond the creation of rules and includes continuous monitoring and auditing. Regular reviews of firewall logs and rule effectiveness are essential to identify anomalies, potential threats, and areas where rule optimization is needed. Auditing firewall rules helps maintain a robust security posture and adapt to the ever-changing threat landscape. In summary, firewall rules and policies are the backbone of network security, defining the boundaries and permissions that govern data traffic within a network. Effective rule management, including thoughtful organization, rule sequencing, and ongoing monitoring, is essential for maintaining a secure and resilient network environment. Firewalls, when configured and managed with care, play a crucial role in safeguarding networks against cyber threats and unauthorized access, enabling organizations to operate with confidence in the digital age.*

*In the vast landscape of network security and privacy, Virtual Private Networks, or VPNs, have emerged as powerful tools for safeguarding digital communication and protecting sensitive data. VPNs are essential in a world where information flows freely across the internet, and the need for secure, private, and anonymous online experiences has never been greater. VPN technologies encompass a wide range of approaches and protocols, each designed to address specific security and privacy requirements. One of the most common VPN types is the remote access VPN, which enables individual users or devices to securely connect to a private network over the internet. Remote access VPNs are widely used by remote workers, travelers, and telecommuters to access corporate resources, such as files and applications, while maintaining the confidentiality and integrity of data. These VPNs employ secure tunneling protocols, like Point-to-Point Tunneling Protocol (PPTP), Layer 2 Tunneling Protocol (L2TP), or Secure Socket Tunneling Protocol (SSTP), to create encrypted connections between remote users and the private network. Site-to-site VPNs, on the other hand, connect entire networks or branch offices to create a secure network-to-network communication channel. Site-to-site VPNs are commonly employed by organizations with multiple locations to establish secure and continuous connectivity between their geographically dispersed networks. These VPNs use tunneling protocols like IPsec (Internet Protocol Security) or Generic Routing Encapsulation (GRE) to create secure tunnels between* routers or gateways at each site, ensuring the confidentiality and integrity of data as it traverses the public internet. Beyond remote access and site-to-site VPNs, there are also specialized VPN technologies designed for specific use cases. One such technology is the SSL VPN (Secure Socket Layer VPN) or TLS VPN (Transport Layer Security VPN), which leverages the SSL/TLS protocols commonly used for securing web traffic. SSL VPNs provide secure remote access to web-based applications and resources through a web browser, eliminating the need for specialized client software. Users can access internal web applications securely without exposing sensitive data to potential threats on public networks. Another specialized VPN technology is the MPLS VPN (Multiprotocol Label Switching VPN), which is often used by service providers to offer secure, private, and scalable communication solutions to their customers. MPLS VPNs enable service providers to create virtual private networks over a shared infrastructure, isolating customer traffic from one another while maintaining efficient routing and traffic engineering. In addition to these VPN types, there are two primary categories of VPN technologies: those that use tunneling protocols and those that use encryption methods. Tunneling protocols encapsulate and route data traffic through secure tunnels, while encryption methods encode the data to protect its confidentiality. Common tunneling protocols used in VPNs include PPTP, L2TP, SSTP, and IPsec, each with its strengths and weaknesses. PPTP, for instance, is known for its simplicity and ease of setup but may have security vulnerabilities. L2TP offers strong security and is often used with IPsec for added encryption but can be more complex to configure. SSTP is a Microsoft-developed protocol that works well in situations where network access is restricted but may not be as widely supported as other protocols. IPsec is a versatile protocol suite that can provide both tunneling and encryption capabilities, making it a popular choice for securing VPN connections. Encryption methods, on the other hand, use cryptographic algorithms to scramble data, rendering it unreadable to unauthorized parties. Common encryption methods include DES (Data Encryption Standard), 3DES (Triple Data Encryption Standard), AES (Advanced Encryption Standard), and RSA (Rivest–Shamir–Adleman). AES, in particular, is widely regarded as a robust encryption standard and is commonly used in VPNs to ensure data confidentiality. VPN technologies also vary in terms of the security protocols and authentication mechanisms they employ. Many VPNs use security protocols like PPTP, L2TP, IPsec, or OpenVPN to establish secure connections. Authentication mechanisms include username and password, digital certificates, and two-factor authentication (2FA). Two-factor authentication, in particular, enhances security by requiring users to provide an additional authentication factor beyond just a password. This can include something they know (like a PIN) and something they have (like a mobile app-generated token). Beyond these standard VPN technologies, emerging technologies like WireGuard are gaining attention for their simplicity, speed, and strong security features. WireGuard is designed to be efficient and easy to configure, making it a promising option for both remote access and site-to-site VPNs. Another recent development is the rise of Zero Trust Network Access (ZTNA), which takes a different approach to network security by assuming that no device or user should be trusted by default, even if they are within the corporate network. ZTNA solutions, such as software-defined perimeters (SDPs), provide access control based on identity, context, and device posture, reducing the attack surface and enhancing security. VPN technologies also extend to mobile devices, with mobile VPNs designed to secure communications for smartphones and tablets. These VPNs are crucial for protecting sensitive data when accessing public Wi-Fi networks or conducting business on mobile devices. Mobile VPNs may use protocols like L2TP/IPsec or SSL VPNs to ensure secure communication on mobile platforms. In addition to the various VPN technologies and protocols, choosing the right VPN service provider is a critical decision. VPN service providers offer a range of features, including server locations, encryption strength, logging policies, and pricing models. Selecting a reputable provider that aligns with your specific security and privacy requirements is essential to ensuring a secure VPN experience. In summary, VPN types and technologies are diverse and adaptable, offering a spectrum of options to secure data communication and protect privacy in an increasingly interconnected world. From remote access and site-to-site VPNs to specialized solutions like SSL VPNs and MPLS VPNs, these technologies empower organizations and individuals to safeguard their digital assets and maintain confidentiality in an ever-evolving threat landscape. Understanding the strengths and limitations of each VPN type and technology is crucial for making informed decisions and implementing effective security strategies in today's dynamic digital environment. In the realm of network security and privacy, setting up

VPN connections is a fundamental process that enables individuals and organizations to establish secure, encrypted communication channels over the internet. Setting up a VPN connection involves several key steps, beginning with the selection of a suitable VPN protocol and service provider. The choice of VPN protocol is essential, as it determines the security, performance, and compatibility of the VPN connection. Common VPN protocols include PPTP, L2TP/IPsec, SSTP, IPsec, OpenVPN, and WireGuard, each with its strengths and weaknesses. PPTP, for instance, is known for its ease of setup but may have security vulnerabilities. L2TP/IPsec provides robust security but may be more complex to configure. SSTP is a Microsoft-developed protocol that works well in restricted network access scenarios. IPsec is versatile, providing both tunneling and encryption capabilities. OpenVPN is an open-source and highly configurable protocol known for its security features. WireGuard is an emerging protocol praised for its simplicity and speed. Once a VPN protocol is selected, the next step is to choose a VPN service provider that offers the desired features, server locations, encryption strength, and privacy policies. Numerous VPN service providers are available, ranging from free options to premium services, each catering to different user requirements. It is crucial to research and select a reputable VPN service provider known for its commitment to user privacy and security. After selecting a VPN protocol and service provider, the next step is to configure the VPN connection on the user's device. Most modern operating systems, including Windows, macOS, Linux, iOS, and Android, offer built-in support for various VPN protocols, simplifying the setup process. Users can typically find VPN configuration settings in the device's network or settings menu. The configuration process typically involves entering details provided by the VPN service provider, such as server addresses, authentication credentials, and encryption settings. Once the VPN connection is configured, users can initiate the connection by selecting the VPN profile and establishing the connection through the device's network settings. After a successful connection, all data traffic originating from the device is routed through the VPN tunnel to the VPN server. The VPN server then forwards the traffic to its intended destination, ensuring that it remains encrypted and secure during transit. One of the essential aspects of setting up VPN connections is ensuring that the VPN client and server settings are compatible. Both sides must use the same VPN protocol and encryption settings to establish a successful connection. Incompatibilities can result in connection failures or security vulnerabilities. When setting up a VPN connection, it is essential to consider the server location, as this can impact the connection's performance and the user's online experience. Choosing a VPN server in close proximity to the user's location typically results in faster connection speeds, as there is less network latency. However, users may also opt to connect to servers in other countries to access geo-restricted content or enhance their privacy by masking their true location. Another consideration is the encryption strength used by the VPN protocol. While stronger encryption provides better security, it can also impact connection speed. Users should strike a balance between security and performance by selecting an encryption level that meets their needs. After setting up a VPN connection, it is advisable to perform thorough testing to ensure that the connection is functioning correctly. Users can test the VPN by accessing websites and online services, verifying that their true IP address is concealed, and assessing the connection speed. Testing the VPN connection under different network conditions, such as public Wi-Fi networks or cellular data, is also crucial to ensure its reliability in various scenarios. Additionally, users should check for potential DNS leaks, which can reveal their true IP address despite using a VPN. To prevent DNS leaks, users can configure their device to use the VPN provider's DNS servers or use DNS leak protection features provided by some VPN clients. Managing VPN connections may also involve considerations related to auto-connect and kill switch features. Auto-connect features automatically establish the VPN connection when the device connects to the internet, ensuring that the user remains protected without manual intervention. Kill switch features, on the other hand, block internet access if the VPN connection drops unexpectedly, preventing data from being transmitted outside the VPN tunnel. These features enhance the reliability and security of VPN connections. In addition to configuring VPN connections on individual devices, organizations may also set up VPNs on routers or gateways to provide network-wide VPN access. Router-based VPN configurations allow multiple devices within a local network to benefit from VPN protection without individual device setup. Organizations can also establish site-to-site VPN connections between branch offices or remote locations to create secure, private communication channels. Setting up site-to-site VPNs typically involves configuring VPN-capable routers or gateways at each location to establish secure connections between them. This approach is commonly used to enable seamless and secure communication between geographically dispersed networks. In summary, setting up VPN connections is a vital process for achieving secure and private internet communication. The steps involved include selecting a suitable VPN protocol and service provider, configuring the VPN connection on the user's device, ensuring compatibility between client and server settings, considering server location and encryption strength, conducting thorough testing, and managing features like auto-connect and kill switch. Whether for individual privacy or corporate security, VPN connections play a crucial role in safeguarding data and protecting online identities in an interconnected world.

In the realm of cybersecurity and access control, user authentication methods serve as the first line of defense, ensuring that only authorized individuals gain access to systems, applications, and data. User authentication is a critical component of information security, as it verifies the identity of users and safeguards against unauthorized access, data breaches, and cyberattacks. The diversity of user authentication methods reflects the evolving landscape of technology and security challenges, offering a range of options to suit various needs and use cases. One of the most traditional and widely used authentication methods is the username and password combination. This method requires users to enter a unique username and a secret password known only to them during the authentication process. Username and password authentication is straightforward and familiar but can be vulnerable to attacks such as brute force attempts and password guessing. To enhance security, organizations often enforce password complexity requirements and periodic password changes. Multi-factor authentication (MFA) is a robust user authentication method that combines two or more authentication factors to verify a user's identity. These factors typically fall into three categories: something the user knows (knowledge factor), something the user has (possession factor), and something the user is (inherence factor). Knowledge factors include passwords, PINs, and security questions, while possession factors encompass items like hardware tokens, smart cards, or mobile devices. Inherence factors involve biometric data, such as fingerprints, facial recognition, or retina scans. MFA enhances security by requiring attackers to compromise multiple factors, making it significantly more challenging for unauthorized individuals to gain access. Biometric authentication methods have gained popularity for their convenience and strong security. Biometric authentication relies on unique physical or behavioral characteristics to verify a user's identity. Common biometric methods include fingerprint recognition, facial recognition, iris scanning, and voice recognition. Biometric data is difficult to replicate, providing a high level of security. However, biometric authentication is not immune to potential risks, such as spoofing attacks using fake fingerprints or facial images. Smart cards and tokens are physical devices that users carry to authenticate themselves. Smart cards typically contain a microchip that stores cryptographic keys or certificates, while tokens generate one-time passwords (OTPs) that change periodically. These devices provide an additional layer of security, as attackers would need physical possession of the card or token to impersonate the user. Single sign-on (SSO) is an authentication method that allows users to access multiple applications and services with a single set of credentials. Once authenticated, users can move seamlessly between different systems without the need to enter their username and password repeatedly. SSO simplifies user access and reduces the risk of password-related security incidents. OAuth and OpenID Connect are popular protocols used for implementing SSO across various web applications and services. Risk-based authentication (RBA) is an adaptive authentication method that evaluates the risk associated with each authentication attempt. RBA assesses various factors, such as the user's location, device, behavior, and transaction context, to determine the level of risk. Based on this assessment, RBA can request additional authentication factors for high-risk activities while allowing low-risk access with minimal friction. RBA helps strike a balance between security and user experience. Time-based one-time passwords (TOTPs) and mobile authentication apps are increasingly used for secure user authentication. TOTPs generate temporary codes that change at fixed intervals, typically every 30 seconds. Users synchronize their TOTP generator (e.g., Google Authenticator) with a service, which then verifies the code during authentication. Mobile authentication apps like Duo and Authy provide similar functionality and can also support push notifications for seamless authentication. Certificate-based authentication relies on digital certificates issued to users or devices. These certificates are used to verify the authenticity of the user or device during authentication. Public key infrastructure (PKI) is often employed to manage and distribute digital certificates securely. Certificate-based authentication is common in enterprise environments and is particularly effective for securing communications within organizations. Behavioral biometrics analyze user behavior patterns, such as typing speed, mouse movements, or touchscreen interactions, to authenticate users. These patterns are unique to individuals and can serve as additional authentication factors. Behavioral biometrics can provide continuous authentication, monitoring user behavior throughout a session to detect anomalies or unauthorized access. Social login, also known as federated authentication, allows users to log in to websites and services using their social media accounts (e.g., Facebook, Google, or LinkedIn). This method simplifies the registration and login process for users, as they can use existing credentials from trusted providers. However, social login raises privacy considerations, as it involves sharing user data with the social media platform. Knowledge-based authentication (KBA) relies on users' knowledge of specific information, such as personal identification questions (PIQs) or shared secrets. Users answer predefined questions or provide secret information during the authentication process. KBA is commonly used for account recovery or identity verification when other authentication methods are not available. Self-sovereign identity (SSI) is an emerging authentication approach that gives individuals control over their own digital identities. SSI allows users to create, own, and manage their digital identity credentials, reducing reliance on centralized identity providers. Blockchain technology is often leveraged to secure SSI systems. Authentication standards and protocols play a crucial role in ensuring interoperability and security. Standards like OAuth 2.0, OpenID Connect, SAML (Security Assertion Markup Language), and FIDO (Fast Identity Online) facilitate secure authentication and authorization across various applications and services. In summary, user authentication methods are diverse and continually evolving to address the complex challenges of cybersecurity and identity management. From traditional username and password combinations to advanced multi-factor authentication, biometrics, and adaptive authentication, these methods provide a spectrum of options to meet varying security and *usability requirements. Selecting the appropriate authentication method depends on factors such as security needs, user experience, and the specific use case at hand. Understanding the strengths and limitations of each method is crucial for organizations and individuals seeking to protect digital identities and sensitive data in an interconnected and dynamic digital landscape. In the realm of information security, access control and permissions are fundamental concepts that govern how individuals and systems interact with data, resources, and applications within an organization. Access control refers to the mechanisms and policies that determine who is allowed to access specific resources and what actions they are permitted to perform. Effective access control is essential for protecting sensitive information, preventing unauthorized access, and maintaining the confidentiality, integrity, and availability of data. Access control is a multifaceted discipline encompassing various components, including authentication, authorization, and auditing. Authentication is the process of verifying the identity of users or systems attempting to access resources. It ensures that individuals or entities are who they claim to be before granting access. Authentication methods can range from simple username and password combinations to more advanced multi-factor authentication (MFA) mechanisms, such as biometrics or smart cards. Authorization, on the other hand, focuses on determining the level of access or permissions granted to authenticated users or systems. It specifies what actions a user or system can perform, which resources they can access, and under what conditions. Authorization mechanisms rely on policies, roles, and permissions that define access rights and restrictions for different user groups or roles within an organization. Auditing is the process of monitoring and recording access events and activities to track who accessed what, when, and how. Auditing plays a crucial role in maintaining accountability, detecting security breaches, and ensuring compliance with regulatory requirements. Access control models provide a framework for implementing access control mechanisms and defining how permissions are managed. Common access control models include discretionary access control (DAC), mandatory access control (MAC), role-based access control (RBAC), and attribute-based access control (ABAC). Discretionary access control (DAC) allows resource owners to define access permissions and determine who can access their resources. It gives users significant control over access but can lead to security risks if permissions are not managed rigorously. Mandatory access control (MAC) enforces access policies based on security labels or classifications assigned to resources and users. It is commonly used in government and military contexts to ensure strict data confidentiality and integrity. Role-based access control (RBAC) assigns permissions to predefined roles or job functions, simplifying access management and reducing the complexity of individual user permissions. RBAC is widely used in organizations to streamline access control administration. Attribute-based access control (ABAC) considers various attributes, such as user attributes, resource attributes, and environmental attributes, to make access decisions. ABAC provides fine-grained control over access and is suitable for complex authorization scenarios. Access control lists (ACLs) and capability lists are practical implementations of access control mechanisms. Access* control lists (ACLs) specify which users or groups have permission to access or modify resources and what actions they can perform. Capability lists, on the other hand, grant users specific capabilities or tokens that enable them to access resources. Both ACLs and capability lists are used to enforce access control policies at the resource level. Access control policies are essential for defining and managing access control rules within an organization. Policies outline who can access what resources, what actions are allowed or denied, and under what conditions access is granted. Well-defined access control policies are crucial for maintaining security and compliance. Access control policies can be static or dynamic. Static policies define access rules that remain constant over time, while dynamic policies adapt to changing conditions or contexts. Dynamic policies may incorporate attributes like user location, time of access, or user behavior to make access decisions. Implementing access control requires the integration of access control mechanisms into the organization's IT infrastructure. Access control mechanisms can be implemented at various layers, including the network, application, and data layers. Network-level access control involves securing network resources, such as firewalls, routers, and switches, to control access to network segments and services. Application-level access control focuses on securing applications and services by implementing authentication and authorization mechanisms within the software. Data-level access control protects data resources by enforcing permissions at the data storage or file system level. Access control can also be applied to cloud environments, where cloud providers offer access management tools and *services to protect cloud resources. Access control extends to user management and user provisioning, ensuring that only authorized users are granted access to systems and resources. User provisioning involves creating, modifying, and deleting user accounts, as well as managing their access rights based on their roles and responsibilities. Effective access control requires ongoing monitoring, assessment, and auditing to detect and respond to security incidents, policy violations, or unauthorized access. Access control logs and audit trails capture access events and user activities, allowing organizations to investigate incidents, track compliance, and improve security policies. In summary, access control and permissions are foundational components of information security, serving as the gatekeepers that safeguard data and resources from unauthorized access and misuse. Access control encompasses authentication, authorization, and auditing, with various models and mechanisms available to enforce access policies. Access control policies, whether static or dynamic, provide the guidelines for defining who can access what and under what conditions. Implementing access control requires integrating mechanisms at multiple layers and managing user provisioning. Ongoing monitoring and auditing are essential for maintaining security and compliance, ensuring that access control remains effective in protecting sensitive information in a rapidly evolving digital landscape.*

*In the ever-evolving landscape of cybersecurity, intrusion detection concepts are crucial for identifying and mitigating threats to computer systems, networks, and data. Intrusion detection is the process of monitoring and analyzing system and network activities to detect and respond to unauthorized or malicious activities. It plays a vital role in maintaining the security and integrity of digital assets, helping organizations stay one step ahead of cyber threats. Intrusion detection systems (IDS) and intrusion prevention systems (IPS) are essential tools in the fight against cyber threats. An IDS is designed to detect and alert on suspicious or unauthorized activities, while an IPS goes a step further by actively blocking or preventing such activities. There are two primary types of intrusion detection: host-based intrusion detection (HIDS) and network-based intrusion detection (NIDS). HIDS focuses on monitoring and analyzing activities on a single host or device, such as a server or workstation. It looks for signs of unauthorized access, system anomalies, or suspicious behavior at the host level. NIDS, on the other hand, is designed to monitor network traffic and detect malicious activity occurring on the network. NIDS sensors are strategically placed throughout the network to analyze traffic and identify potential threats. Intrusion detection relies on a set of predefined rules or signatures to identify known attack patterns or indicators of compromise (IoCs). These rules are created based on the characteristics and behaviors associated with specific threats. When network* or system activity matches a rule's criteria, an alert is generated, notifying security personnel of a potential intrusion or security event. Signature-based intrusion detection is effective at identifying known threats but may struggle with detecting new or zero-day attacks for which there are no predefined signatures. To address this limitation, anomaly-based intrusion detection employs machine learning and behavioral analysis to identify deviations from established baselines of normal behavior. Anomaly-based IDS systems learn and adapt to the network's typical traffic patterns and raise alerts when deviations from the norm are detected. This approach can help identify previously unknown threats and unusual behaviors that may indicate an intrusion. Intrusion detection is not limited to real-time monitoring; it also includes retrospective analysis. Security information and event management (SIEM) systems collect and store logs and data from various sources, enabling organizations to perform post-incident investigations and forensic analysis. Intrusion detection systems can be classified as passive or active. Passive IDS systems monitor and analyze traffic or activities without actively intervening or blocking anything. They generate alerts and reports for human intervention or further analysis. Active IDS systems, on the other hand, can take automated actions to respond to detected threats, such as blocking malicious IP addresses or isolating compromised systems. While active IDS systems offer the advantage of immediate threat mitigation, they should be carefully configured to avoid inadvertently disrupting legitimate traffic. Intrusion detection can be implemented using a combination of hardware and software solutions. Hardware-based IDS devices, known as intrusion detection appliances, are dedicated devices designed to monitor and analyze network traffic. Software-based IDS solutions, on the other hand, are applications or programs that run on existing hardware and can be installed on servers or network devices. Hybrid approaches combine both hardware and software components to provide comprehensive intrusion detection capabilities. Intrusion detection is an integral part of a layered security strategy, working alongside other security measures such as firewalls, antivirus software, and access control. Effective intrusion detection requires regular updates of signatures and rules to stay current with emerging threats and vulnerabilities. Continuous monitoring and analysis of alerts and events are essential to reduce false positives and investigate potential incidents. Threat intelligence feeds and collaboration with cybersecurity communities and information-sharing organizations can provide valuable insights into the latest threats and attack vectors. Intrusion detection is not a one-size-fits-all solution; it should be tailored to an organization's specific needs and risk profile. Organizations must consider factors such as the size and complexity of their network, the types of assets they need to protect, and their compliance requirements when implementing an intrusion detection strategy. Intrusion detection is a proactive approach to cybersecurity, allowing organizations to detect and respond to threats before they escalate into more significant security incidents. It provides an essential layer of defense, helping organizations safeguard their digital assets, maintain regulatory compliance, and protect their reputation in the face of evolving cyber threats. Intrusion detection concepts and technologies continue to evolve to keep pace with the ever-changing threat landscape, making it a critical component of modern cybersecurity strategies. System hardening techniques are fundamental strategies used to enhance the security of computer systems, servers, and network devices, reducing their susceptibility to cyber threats and attacks. System hardening involves configuring and managing various aspects of a system to minimize vulnerabilities, limit potential attack vectors, and ensure that security controls are in place. One of the fundamental principles of system hardening is reducing the attack surface, which refers to the potential points of entry or exploitation that an attacker can target. To achieve this, unnecessary services, applications, and protocols should be disabled or removed from the system. This minimizes the exposure to potential vulnerabilities and reduces the complexity of the system, making it easier to manage and secure. Disabling unused ports and services, such as FTP or Telnet, helps prevent attackers from exploiting known vulnerabilities in these services. Another essential aspect of system hardening is keeping the system's software and firmware up to date. Regularly applying security patches, updates, and firmware upgrades is crucial to address known vulnerabilities and weaknesses. Outdated software can be a prime target for attackers looking to exploit known flaws. Patch management processes should be well-defined and include testing and validation before deploying updates to production systems. System hardening often involves strengthening authentication mechanisms to prevent unauthorized access. Enforcing strong password policies, implementing multi-factor *authentication (MFA), and disabling default accounts and passwords are common practices. Limiting user privileges through the principle of least privilege (PoLP) ensures that users and processes have only the minimum access necessary to perform their tasks. This minimizes the potential damage that can be caused in the event of a security breach. Access controls, such as access control lists (ACLs) and role-based access control (RBAC), play a crucial role in system hardening. By configuring granular access controls, organizations can restrict access to sensitive data and resources. Firewalls and intrusion detection/prevention systems (IDS/IPS) are key components of system hardening. Firewalls filter incoming and outgoing network traffic, allowing organizations to define rules and policies that specify which traffic is allowed or blocked. IDS/IPS systems monitor network and system activities for suspicious or malicious behavior, alerting administrators to potential security incidents. Encryption is a critical system hardening technique for protecting data in transit and at rest. Implementing encryption protocols such as SSL/TLS for web traffic and encrypting sensitive files and databases helps safeguard data from interception and unauthorized access. Regular system backups and disaster recovery planning are essential for system hardening. In the event of a security incident or system compromise, having up-to-date backups ensures that data can be restored, minimizing downtime and data loss. System hardening extends to physical security measures. Securing server rooms, data centers, and hardware assets against physical threats is as important as protecting against digital threats. Implementing access controls, surveillance, and environmental monitoring helps safeguard critical infrastructure. Auditing and monitoring are ongoing processes in system hardening. Logging system and network events, analyzing logs, and setting up alerts for suspicious activities enable organizations to detect and respond to security incidents promptly. Security Information and Event Management (SIEM) systems are valuable tools for centralizing and analyzing log data. Vulnerability scanning and penetration testing are proactive system hardening techniques. Regular vulnerability scans identify potential weaknesses, allowing organizations to address them before attackers can exploit them. Penetration testing simulates real-world attacks to assess the effectiveness of security controls and discover vulnerabilities. Compliance with industry standards and regulations, such as the Payment Card Industry Data Security Standard (PCI DSS) or the Health Insurance Portability and Accountability Act (HIPAA), is a critical aspect of system hardening for organizations subject to specific requirements. Adhering to these standards ensures that security measures are in place to protect sensitive data and maintain regulatory compliance. System hardening should be an ongoing and iterative process. Regularly reviewing and updating security policies, configurations, and controls is essential to adapt to evolving threats and vulnerabilities. Training and educating personnel about security best practices and the importance of system hardening contribute to a security-aware culture within organizations. In summary, system hardening techniques are essential for enhancing the security of computer systems, servers, and network devices. By reducing the attack surface, keeping software up to date, enforcing strong authentication, implementing access controls, using firewalls and intrusion detection systems, encrypting data, and following best practices, organizations can significantly improve their resilience against cyber threats. System hardening is an ongoing effort that requires continuous monitoring, auditing, and adaptation to ensure that systems remain secure in the face of an ever-changing threat landscape.*

*Security policies and procedures are the foundation of any organization's efforts to establish and maintain a robust cybersecurity posture. These documents provide a structured framework for managing security risks, protecting sensitive information, and ensuring compliance with regulatory requirements. Security policies are high-level documents that outline an organization's overarching security objectives, principles, and strategic goals. They define the organization's commitment to security, its approach to risk management, and its dedication to safeguarding information assets. Security procedures, on the other hand, are detailed guidelines and step-by-step instructions that specify how security-related tasks and activities should be carried out. These procedures translate the principles and goals outlined in security policies into practical actions and processes. The development and implementation of security policies and procedures are essential for creating a security-conscious culture within an organization. These documents serve as a reference point for employees, contractors, and third parties, helping them understand their roles and responsibilities in maintaining security. Security policies typically encompass various areas of security, including information security, physical security, access control, and incident response. Information security policies address the protection of digital assets, data, and information systems. They define acceptable use policies, data classification and handling guidelines, and requirements for encryption, access control, and data retention. Physical security policies focus on securing physical assets, facilities, and infrastructure. They detail access control measures, visitor management, surveillance, and disaster recovery procedures for physical incidents. Access control policies specify how user access to systems, applications, and data should be managed. These policies include user account management, authentication methods, password policies, and authorization rules. Incident response policies outline the organization's procedures for detecting, reporting, and responding to security incidents. They define roles and responsibilities within the incident response team and provide guidelines for handling different types of incidents. Security policies and procedures should be tailored to the organization's specific needs, risks, and regulatory requirements. They should be reviewed and updated regularly to stay current with evolving security threats and changes in the business environment. To ensure the effectiveness of security policies and procedures, organizations must promote awareness and education among employees. Security awareness programs help employees understand the importance of security, recognize potential threats, and adhere to security policies and procedures. Training and education programs should be designed to keep employees informed about emerging threats and best practices. Security policies and procedures play a crucial role in achieving compliance with industry regulations and standards. Many regulatory frameworks, such as the General Data Protection Regulation (GDPR) and the Health Insurance Portability and Accountability Act (HIPAA), require organizations to have comprehensive security policies and procedures in place. Compliance with these regulations helps organizations avoid legal and financial consequences while enhancing data protection and privacy practices. The process of developing security policies and procedures typically involves multiple stakeholders within the organization. It is essential to engage various departments, including IT, legal, human resources, and compliance, to ensure that the documents align with the organization's goals and objectives. Security policies and procedures should be communicated effectively to all relevant parties. This includes employees, contractors, vendors, and anyone who interacts with the organization's systems and data. Clear communication ensures that individuals understand their responsibilities and obligations regarding security. Auditing and monitoring are critical components of security policy and procedure management. Organizations should regularly assess compliance with their policies and procedures through audits and security assessments. Monitoring tools and practices should be in place to detect and respond to policy violations or security incidents. In cases of non-compliance or security breaches, organizations must have procedures in place for investigation, mitigation, and reporting. Security policies and procedures are not static documents; they require regular review and updates. As technology evolves and new threats emerge, organizations need to adapt their policies to address these changes. Regular reviews also help identify areas where policies may be overly restrictive or where procedures can be streamlined for efficiency. In summary, security policies and procedures are essential elements of a comprehensive cybersecurity strategy. These documents provide the framework for defining security objectives, outlining* responsibilities, and establishing guidelines for protecting information and assets. By developing, implementing, and maintaining effective security policies and procedures, organizations can create a security-conscious culture, ensure regulatory compliance, and respond effectively to security incidents in an ever-changing threat landscape. Security policies and procedures serve as the backbone of an organization's cybersecurity efforts, providing a structured framework for safeguarding sensitive information and managing security risks. These documents are instrumental in defining the organization's commitment to security, outlining its strategic goals, and establishing a clear set of principles that guide security-related decisions and actions. Security policies, in essence, articulate the high-level security objectives of the organization, setting the tone for the entire security program and conveying the organization's unwavering dedication to protecting its information assets.

Within the realm of security policies, one can identify various categories, each addressing specific aspects of security governance. Information security policies, for instance, lay down the guidelines and rules for securing digital assets, data, and information systems. These policies encompass a range of topics, including data classification and handling, acceptable use of assets, encryption requirements, and access control mechanisms. By defining these aspects, information security policies establish the groundwork for robust data protection strategies and ensure that employees are aware of their responsibilities in safeguarding sensitive information.

Physical security policies, on the other hand, focus on the safeguarding of tangible assets, facilities, and *infrastructure. These policies delve into the realms of access control, visitor management, surveillance, and disaster recovery procedures for physical incidents. By defining measures for securing premises and controlling access to sensitive areas, physical security policies contribute to a comprehensive security posture that extends beyond the digital realm.*

*Access control policies play a pivotal role in governing how user access to systems, applications, and data is managed within an organization. These policies encompass a wide array of considerations, ranging from user account management and authentication mechanisms to password policies and authorization rules. Access control policies work in tandem with other security measures to ensure that only authorized individuals have access to specific resources, reducing the risk of unauthorized data exposure or system compromise.*

*Incident response policies form yet another critical component of security policies and procedures. These policies outline the organization's procedures for detecting, reporting, and responding to security incidents. They establish the framework for creating and maintaining an incident response team, define roles and responsibilities, and provide guidance on handling various types of incidents. By having these policies in place, organizations can swiftly and effectively mitigate security breaches, minimizing the potential impact on their operations and reputation.*

*Security policies and procedures should be meticulously crafted to align with the organization's unique needs, risk profile, and regulatory obligations. They should be rooted in an understanding of the specific threats and* vulnerabilities that the organization faces, taking into account the industry it operates in and the nature of its business. By customizing these documents to suit their context, organizations can ensure that their security measures are both robust and relevant.

To maintain the effectiveness of security policies and procedures, organizations must cultivate a culture of security awareness among their employees. Security awareness programs are designed to educate staff members about the importance of security, familiarize them with potential threats, and promote adherence to security policies and procedures. These programs serve as a frontline defense, empowering employees to recognize and respond to security risks in their day-to-day activities.

Effective communication of security policies and procedures is essential to ensure that everyone within the organization is well-informed and understands their role in maintaining security. Policies should be readily accessible to all employees, contractors, and third parties who interact with the organization's systems and data. Clear communication helps to prevent misunderstandings and ensures that individuals are aware of their responsibilities regarding security.

Auditing and monitoring are integral components of security policy and procedure management. Organizations should regularly assess their compliance with these documents through audits and security assessments. Monitoring tools and practices should be in place to detect policy violations or security incidents promptly. In cases of non-compliance or security breaches, organizations must have well-defined procedures for investigation, mitigation, and reporting.

*Security policies and procedures are not static; they require ongoing review and updates. The dynamic nature of technology and evolving threats necessitate regular evaluations to ensure that policies remain effective. Regular reviews also help identify areas where policies may need adjustment or streamlining for efficiency.*

*In summary, security policies and procedures are the cornerstone of a robust cybersecurity strategy. These documents provide a structured framework for defining security objectives, outlining responsibilities, and establishing guidelines for protecting information and assets. By developing, implementing, and maintaining effective security policies and procedures, organizations can create a security-aware culture, ensure regulatory compliance, and respond effectively to security incidents in an ever-changing threat landscape.*

## Chapter 9: Network Services Configuration

DNS (Domain Name System) configuration and management are integral components of modern network administration, serving as the backbone of the internet by translating human-readable domain names into IP addresses that computers use to locate resources on the web. Proper DNS configuration ensures that network resources are accessible, and domain names resolve accurately, allowing users to reach websites, send emails, and access various online services seamlessly.

At its core, DNS is a distributed hierarchical system, organized into zones and records. DNS zones are administrative domains for which a specific entity is responsible, such as example.com or openai.org. Within each zone, DNS records hold essential information like IP addresses, mail server destinations (MX records), and alias records (CNAME) that point to other domain names. DNS configuration starts with the creation and management of these records within the DNS server.

DNS servers come in two primary flavors: authoritative and recursive. Authoritative DNS servers are responsible for storing and serving DNS records for specific zones. Organizations typically have their authoritative DNS servers to manage their domain names. Recursive DNS servers, on the other hand, resolve DNS queries on behalf of clients by recursively querying authoritative servers to find the IP address associated with a given domain name.

To configure DNS, network administrators need to define and maintain resource records within authoritative DNS servers. These records include A (Address) records, which map domain names to IPv4 addresses, and AAAA records, which perform the same function for IPv6 addresses. MX (Mail Exchange) records specify email servers responsible for receiving emails on behalf of a domain. CNAME (Canonical Name) records create aliases for domain names, allowing multiple names to point to the same IP address. TXT records hold arbitrary text data and are often used for verification and security purposes, such as SPF (Sender Policy Framework) records for email authentication.

DNS configuration is a dynamic process that requires continuous management. As organizations grow and change, their DNS records must be updated to reflect alterations in infrastructure, server locations, and service providers. Failing to maintain accurate DNS records can result in service disruptions and accessibility issues for users.

DNS cache management is another critical aspect of DNS configuration. DNS resolvers, which are typically operated by internet service providers (ISPs) or organizations, maintain caches of DNS records to reduce the time and resources required to resolve common queries. Cache management strategies involve setting Time to Live (TTL) values in DNS records, which determine how long records should be cached by resolvers. Proper TTL settings balance the need for fast, up-to-date DNS resolution with minimizing the load on authoritative servers.

DNS Security Extensions (DNSSEC) play a vital role in DNS configuration and management. DNSSEC is a suite of extensions that adds cryptographic authentication to DNS, ensuring the integrity and authenticity of DNS records. It guards against DNS cache poisoning attacks, which can lead to incorrect DNS resolutions and potential security breaches. Implementing DNSSEC involves signing DNS zones with digital signatures and configuring DNS resolvers to verify these signatures.

Redundancy and high availability are essential considerations in DNS configuration and management. Organizations often deploy multiple authoritative DNS servers, distributed across different geographic locations, to ensure DNS services remain accessible even in the face of server failures or network issues. Load balancing solutions can distribute DNS queries across these servers, optimizing performance and minimizing downtime.

Another important DNS management task is monitoring and analytics. Administrators should regularly monitor DNS server performance, query traffic, and resolution times to identify potential issues and bottlenecks. DNS logs and analytics tools can provide insights into DNS-related incidents and help troubleshoot problems.

As part of DNS management, administrators should also stay informed about DNS threats and vulnerabilities. DNS attacks, such as Distributed Denial of Service (DDoS) attacks and cache poisoning attacks, can disrupt services and compromise security. Implementing security measures, such as rate limiting, firewall rules, and intrusion detection systems, can help mitigate these threats.

In summary, DNS configuration and management are vital components of network administration and cybersecurity. Proper configuration ensures that domain names are resolved accurately, allowing users to access resources on the internet. It involves the creation and maintenance of DNS records, accurate TTL settings, cache management, and the implementation of security measures like DNSSEC. Redundancy, load balancing, and monitoring are crucial for ensuring DNS availability and performance. Administrators must also stay vigilant against DNS-related threats and vulnerabilities to maintain the integrity and security of their DNS infrastructure.

Dynamic Host Configuration Protocol (DHCP) and IP addressing are fundamental elements of modern networking, playing a pivotal role in ensuring the seamless communication of devices within both local and global networks. DHCP, in particular, simplifies the process of IP address assignment and management, enabling network administrators to efficiently allocate and manage IP addresses across their networks.

IP addressing, the cornerstone of network communication, provides a unique identity to every device connected to a network, allowing data packets to be routed accurately from source to destination. IP addresses are classified into two major categories: IPv4 (Internet Protocol version 4) and IPv6 (Internet Protocol version 6). IPv4, the older and more widely used protocol, employs a 32-bit address format, while IPv6 utilizes a 128-bit address format to accommodate the ever-expanding number of devices on the internet.

Within the IPv4 address space, IP addresses are divided into several classes, such as Class A, Class B, and Class C, each with a different range of available addresses. Classful addressing, however, has largely been replaced by Classless Inter-Domain Routing (CIDR), a more flexible approach that allows for the efficient allocation of IP addresses based on network requirements.

IP addresses can be either static or dynamic. Static IP addresses are manually configured, typically assigned to servers, network devices, and infrastructure components that require a permanent, unchanging address. Conversely, dynamic IP addresses are automatically assigned by DHCP servers on the network, offering a more flexible and scalable approach to IP address management.

The DHCP protocol serves as the cornerstone of dynamic IP address assignment, simplifying the process of configuring networked devices and reducing the administrative burden of manually configuring IP addresses. DHCP operates using a client-server model, where DHCP servers are responsible for leasing IP addresses and configuration information to DHCP clients.

When a DHCP client joins a network, it sends a DHCP discovery request to locate available DHCP servers. DHCP servers respond by offering IP addresses and configuration settings, including subnet masks, default gateways, DNS server addresses, and more. The client then selects an offer and sends a DHCP request to formally request the offered IP address and configuration parameters.

Upon receiving the DHCP request, the DHCP server acknowledges the lease and provides the client with an IP address lease duration. The client is responsible for renewing the lease before it expires or requesting a new lease if it moves to a different network segment.

DHCP simplifies IP address management by allowing administrators to centralize the assignment and configuration of IP addresses. This centralization reduces the likelihood of address conflicts, simplifies network reconfiguration, and ensures efficient use of available IP addresses.

Furthermore, DHCP supports various deployment scenarios, including single DHCP servers, redundant DHCP servers for high availability, and DHCP relay agents that facilitate DHCP communication across different network segments. These options provide flexibility in tailoring DHCP to the specific needs of an organization's network infrastructure.

DHCP supports the use of IP address pools, allowing administrators to define ranges of IP addresses that can be leased to clients. This ensures that addresses are allocated efficiently and avoids IP address exhaustion. Lease durations can be configured to meet organizational requirements, with shorter leases providing more dynamic address assignment and longer leases reducing DHCP traffic.

To enhance security and network management, DHCP can be integrated with authentication mechanisms. This ensures that only authorized clients receive IP address assignments. By employing authentication, organizations can enforce access controls and prevent unauthorized devices from connecting to the network.

Dynamic DNS (DDNS) is often used in conjunction with DHCP to automatically update DNS records when clients receive new IP address assignments. This integration simplifies the process of keeping DNS records accurate, allowing users to access networked resources by hostname rather than IP address.

When managing DHCP, administrators should consider IP address reservation, a feature that assigns specific IP addresses to particular clients based on their unique identifiers, such as MAC addresses. Reserved IP addresses ensure that critical devices always receive the same address, simplifying network management.

Additionally, subnetting, a technique that divides an IP network into smaller, more manageable segments, plays a significant role in IP address management. Subnetting optimizes network performance and allows for efficient IP address allocation within an organization.

In summary, DHCP and IP addressing are essential components of modern networking, enabling the efficient allocation and management of IP addresses within both local and global networks. DHCP simplifies the configuration of networked devices, reduces administrative overhead, and supports various deployment scenarios. By integrating DHCP with authentication and DDNS, organizations can enhance security and simplify network management. Proper IP address management, including techniques like subnetting and IP address reservation, ensures efficient use of IP address resources and optimal network performance.

## Chapter 10: Advanced Security Techniques and Strategies

Encryption and cryptography form the bedrock of modern information security, providing the means to protect sensitive data from unauthorized access and ensure the confidentiality, integrity, and authenticity of digital communications.

At its core, encryption is the process of converting plain, readable text, known as plaintext, into an unreadable format, known as ciphertext, using algorithms and cryptographic keys. Encryption serves as a protective shield that obscures the meaning of data, rendering it indecipherable to anyone without the appropriate decryption key.

Cryptography, the science behind encryption, encompasses a wide range of techniques and mathematical principles designed to secure information. Throughout history, cryptography has played a vital role in securing military communications, financial transactions, and personal messages, dating back to ancient civilizations.

Modern encryption relies on sophisticated mathematical algorithms, classified into two main categories: symmetric-key encryption and asymmetric-key encryption. Symmetric-key encryption employs a single key for both encryption and decryption, making it faster and more efficient. However, the challenge lies in securely distributing the key to all parties involved.

Asymmetric-key encryption, also known as public-key encryption, uses a pair of mathematically related keys: a public key for encryption and a private key for decryption.

This approach addresses the key distribution problem, as the public key can be freely shared while the private key remains confidential.

Public-key infrastructure (PKI) is a critical component of asymmetric encryption, enabling secure communication and digital signatures. PKI relies on trusted third-party entities, known as certificate authorities (CAs), to issue digital certificates that bind public keys to individuals or entities.

One of the most widely used encryption algorithms in symmetric encryption is the Advanced Encryption Standard (AES). AES operates on fixed-size blocks of data, known as blocks ciphers, and supports various key lengths, making it suitable for a wide range of security applications.

Another important symmetric encryption technique is the Data Encryption Standard (DES), although it has largely been replaced by AES due to its vulnerability to brute force attacks.

Asymmetric encryption employs algorithms like RSA (Rivest-Shamir-Adleman) and Elliptic Curve Cryptography (ECC), which are crucial for secure communication over the internet and the protection of digital identities.

Secure Sockets Layer (SSL) and its successor, Transport Layer Security (TLS), are cryptographic protocols that provide secure communication over the internet. They use a combination of symmetric and asymmetric encryption to establish secure connections between clients and servers, ensuring data privacy and integrity during data transmission.

The importance of encryption extends beyond securing data in transit. Data at rest, stored on storage devices or servers, is also vulnerable to unauthorized access. Full-disk encryption (FDE) addresses this concern by encrypting the entire storage medium, rendering the data unreadable without the decryption key.

File-level encryption, another data-at-rest protection method, encrypts individual files or directories, allowing for more granular control over data security.

End-to-end encryption (E2E) is a crucial encryption paradigm for ensuring that only the intended recipients can decrypt and read messages or data. It is commonly used in secure messaging applications and email services to protect the privacy of communications.

Quantum computing poses a potential threat to classical encryption algorithms, as it has the potential to break widely used encryption schemes like RSA and ECC. To counter this threat, researchers are exploring the development of post-quantum cryptography, which aims to create encryption methods resistant to quantum attacks.

In addition to confidentiality, encryption also plays a vital role in ensuring data integrity. Cryptographic hash functions generate fixed-size hash values from arbitrary input data. Hashes are used to verify the integrity of data by comparing the calculated hash value with the expected value. Any alteration to the data, even a single bit, results in a different hash value.

Digital signatures, another cryptographic technique, provide a means of verifying the authenticity and integrity of digital messages or documents. Digital signatures are generated using the sender's private key and can be verified using their public key, ensuring that the content has not been tampered with and that it originates from the claimed sender.

Despite the critical role of encryption in cybersecurity, it is not without challenges and controversies. The use of encryption has sparked debates about the balance between individual privacy and national security. Governments and law enforcement agencies have expressed concerns that strong encryption may hinder their ability to combat criminal activities and terrorism by preventing access to encrypted data.

End-to-end encryption, in particular, has been a subject of debate, as it can impede lawful interception of communications, even with proper legal authorization.

While encryption is a powerful tool for safeguarding data, its effectiveness depends on proper implementation and key management. Weak or misconfigured encryption can lead to vulnerabilities that attackers can exploit. Therefore, organizations must follow best practices for encryption and stay up-to-date with emerging threats and encryption standards.

In summary, encryption and cryptography are essential components of information security, providing the means to protect data confidentiality, integrity, and authenticity. These technologies have evolved significantly, from ancient ciphers to modern encryption algorithms and protocols. Encryption safeguards data in transit and at rest, securing digital communications and protecting sensitive information. As encryption continues to play a vital role in our increasingly digital world, it remains a critical tool for ensuring the privacy and security of individuals and organizations alike.

Security incident response is a critical component of any organization's cybersecurity strategy, serving as the structured approach to managing and mitigating security incidents that threaten the confidentiality, integrity, and availability of data and resources. Incidents come in various forms, including data breaches, malware infections, unauthorized access attempts, and denial-of-service attacks, necessitating a well-defined incident response plan.

The primary goal of incident response is to minimize the impact of security incidents by swiftly identifying, containing, eradicating, and recovering from them. An effective incident response process allows organizations to maintain business continuity, protect sensitive information, and uphold their reputation.

Incident response begins with preparation, where organizations establish an incident response team comprising individuals with diverse skills, including IT, legal, communications, and management. This team is responsible for developing and maintaining the incident response plan, which outlines the procedures and responsibilities for handling security incidents.

To facilitate incident detection, organizations deploy security monitoring and logging solutions that continuously collect and analyze network traffic, system logs, and security events. These tools help identify abnormal activities or indicators of compromise that may signal a security incident.

Once an incident is detected, it is crucial to classify its severity and impact. This classification guides the response effort, determining the level of resources and attention required. Incidents are often categorized as low, medium, or high severity, with corresponding response protocols.

Containment is the immediate action taken to prevent the incident from spreading further and causing additional harm. Depending on the incident, containment measures may involve isolating affected systems, blocking malicious network traffic, or disabling compromised user accounts. The goal is to limit the incident's scope and prevent it from causing more damage.

After containment, organizations focus on eradicating the root cause of the incident. This step involves identifying and removing any malicious software, vulnerabilities, or compromised credentials that allowed the incident to occur. It is essential to ensure that the incident cannot recur.

Recovery efforts aim to restore affected systems and services to normal operation. Organizations may rebuild compromised systems, restore data from backups, and apply necessary patches or updates to prevent similar incidents in the future. Recovery also involves verifying the integrity of systems and data to ensure they are secure.

Communication is a critical aspect of incident response, both internally and externally. Organizations must notify relevant stakeholders, including employees, customers, partners, regulatory authorities, and law enforcement agencies, as required by legal and regulatory obligations. Clear and transparent communication helps manage the incident's impact and maintain trust.

Legal and compliance considerations play a significant role in incident response. Organizations must understand and adhere to data breach notification laws, industry-specific regulations, and contractual obligations that may require reporting incidents to authorities or affected parties. Legal counsel is often involved in guiding these aspects of the response.

Documentation is essential throughout the incident response process. Organizations must maintain detailed records of the incident, including the timeline of events, actions taken, and evidence collected. Proper documentation aids in post-incident analysis, forensic investigations, and potential legal proceedings.

Post-incident analysis is a critical phase of incident response, where organizations assess the incident's causes, impact, and response effectiveness. This analysis helps identify areas for improvement in the incident response plan and the overall security posture. Lessons learned from past incidents inform future incident preparedness.

Continuous improvement is a fundamental principle of incident response. Organizations should regularly review and update their incident response plan, incorporating lessons learned, emerging threats, and changes in technology and business operations. This iterative process enhances the organization's ability to respond effectively to evolving security challenges.

Collaboration with external parties, such as incident response teams, cybersecurity organizations, and information-sharing communities, can enhance incident response capabilities. Sharing threat intelligence and best practices with peers and industry partners helps organizations stay ahead of emerging threats and bolster their defenses.

Incident response is not solely a technical endeavor; it also encompasses the human element. Training and awareness programs educate employees about security policies, procedures, and the role they play in incident response. A well-informed workforce can help detect and report security incidents promptly.

In summary, security incident response is an essential component of cybersecurity, ensuring that organizations can effectively detect, respond to, and recover from security incidents. A well-prepared incident response plan, a skilled response team, effective communication, and continuous improvement are key elements in mitigating the impact of security incidents and maintaining the organization's resilience in the face of evolving threats.

**BOOK 2**
**UNIX AND LINUX SYSTEM ADMINISTRATION HANDBOOK**
**CLOUD INTEGRATION AND INFRASTRUCTURE AS CODE**

**ROB BOTWRIGHT**

## Chapter 1: Introduction to Cloud Computing

Cloud computing has revolutionized the way organizations and individuals access, store, and manage their data and applications by providing a flexible and scalable alternative to traditional on-premises IT infrastructure. At its core, cloud computing is a technology paradigm that leverages the internet to deliver computing resources and services, such as servers, storage, databases, networking, and software, on-demand and as a utility.

The fundamental concept of cloud computing is the delivery of computing resources over the internet, often referred to as "the cloud," where users can access and use these resources without needing to own or maintain physical hardware. Cloud service providers, like Amazon Web Services (AWS), Microsoft Azure, and Google Cloud Platform (GCP), operate vast data centers with a wide range of infrastructure and services that customers can rent or subscribe to.

One of the key advantages of cloud computing is its scalability. Cloud providers offer resources on a pay-as-you-go basis, allowing users to increase or decrease their computing capacity as needed. This elasticity is particularly valuable for organizations with fluctuating workloads, as they can scale up during peak demand and scale down during periods of reduced activity, optimizing resource utilization and cost efficiency.

Cloud computing offers three primary service models: Infrastructure as a Service (IaaS), Platform as a Service (PaaS), and Software as a Service (SaaS). IaaS provides users with virtualized computing resources, including virtual machines, storage, and networking, allowing them to manage and control the underlying infrastructure while maintaining flexibility and scalability.

PaaS offers a higher level of abstraction by providing a platform that includes the underlying infrastructure and development tools, enabling developers to focus on building and deploying applications without worrying about managing the infrastructure's details.

SaaS delivers fully functional software applications over the internet, eliminating the need for users to install, maintain, or update software locally. Common examples of SaaS applications include email services, office productivity suites, and customer relationship management (CRM) software.

Cloud computing deployment models include public cloud, private cloud, and hybrid cloud. Public cloud services are offered and operated by third-party cloud providers, making them accessible to anyone over the internet. Private clouds, on the other hand, are dedicated cloud environments that organizations build and manage for their exclusive use, offering greater control and security.

Hybrid clouds combine elements of both public and private clouds, allowing data and applications to be shared between them. This model provides flexibility and can be ideal for organizations that want to take advantage of the scalability of the public cloud while maintaining sensitive data and critical applications on-premises.

Security is a paramount concern in cloud computing. Cloud providers invest heavily in security measures to protect their infrastructure and customers' data, including physical security, encryption, access controls, and monitoring. However, customers also share responsibility for securing their applications and data in the cloud, requiring a shared security model where both the provider and the customer have roles and responsibilities.

Data privacy and compliance considerations are crucial when using cloud services. Organizations must ensure that they adhere to data protection regulations and industry-specific compliance standards relevant to their operations and the regions in which they operate.

Cloud computing has enabled the proliferation of various cloud-native technologies and practices, such as containerization, serverless computing, and microservices architecture. Containers, powered by technologies like Docker and Kubernetes, offer a lightweight and consistent way to package and deploy applications, making them highly portable and efficient.

Serverless computing allows developers to write and deploy code without managing the underlying infrastructure, enabling automatic scaling based on demand. Microservices architecture involves breaking down complex applications into smaller, loosely coupled services that can be independently developed, deployed, and scaled.

Multi-cloud and edge computing are emerging trends in the cloud computing landscape. Multi-cloud strategies involve using multiple cloud providers to avoid vendor lock-in, increase redundancy, and leverage specialized services from different providers. Edge computing brings compute resources closer to the data source or endpoint devices, reducing latency and enabling real-time processing for applications like IoT and autonomous vehicles.

Cloud computing has had a profound impact on industries, enabling digital transformation, innovation, and agility. It has democratized access to advanced technologies, allowing startups and enterprises alike to compete on a level playing field. Cloud services have become the foundation for a wide range of applications, from e-commerce platforms and streaming services to artificial intelligence and machine learning.

As organizations increasingly rely on cloud computing, there is a growing need for skilled professionals who can design, manage, and secure cloud environments. Cloud certifications and training programs have emerged to meet this demand, helping individuals acquire the knowledge and skills needed to excel in cloud-related roles.

In summary, cloud computing has become a ubiquitous and transformative technology, reshaping the way we access and deliver IT resources and services. Its flexibility, scalability, and cost-efficiency have made it an integral part of modern business and technology landscapes. As cloud computing continues to evolve, organizations must adapt to harness its full potential while addressing the associated challenges of security, compliance, and data management. Cloud adoption offers numerous benefits to organizations but also presents a set of challenges that must be carefully considered and addressed. One of the primary advantages of cloud adoption is the flexibility it provides, allowing organizations to scale resources up or down according to their needs. This scalability enables cost optimization by eliminating the need to maintain on-premises infrastructure that may be underutilized during periods of low demand.

Additionally, cloud computing can significantly reduce capital expenditures, as organizations no longer need to invest in expensive hardware and data center facilities. Instead, they can subscribe to cloud services on a pay-as-you-go basis, shifting from a capital expenditure (CapEx) model to an operational expenditure (OpEx) model.

Another key benefit of cloud adoption is the agility it offers. Organizations can quickly provision and deploy computing resources, reducing the time required to bring new applications and services to market. This agility fosters innovation and competitiveness in a rapidly evolving business landscape.

Moreover, cloud providers offer a wide array of services and tools that can enhance productivity and efficiency. These services include managed databases, serverless computing, artificial intelligence and machine learning capabilities, and more. By leveraging these services, organizations can focus on developing and delivering value-added features instead of managing infrastructure.

Disaster recovery and business continuity are also improved through cloud adoption. Cloud providers typically offer robust backup and data replication options, ensuring data resilience and minimizing downtime in the event of hardware failures or natural disasters. This level of redundancy and data replication is often cost-prohibitive to achieve on-premises.

Collaboration and remote work capabilities are enhanced in a cloud-enabled environment. With cloud-based collaboration tools and communication platforms, employees can collaborate from anywhere, promoting flexibility and remote work arrangements. This capability has become particularly important in recent times, as organizations adapt to remote work trends.

Furthermore, cloud providers invest heavily in security measures, offering robust security services and features that can help organizations protect their data and applications. These security features include identity and access management, encryption, network security, and threat detection.

Despite these advantages, cloud adoption also comes with its set of challenges. One significant challenge is data security and privacy. Entrusting sensitive data to a third-party cloud provider raises concerns about data breaches and compliance with data protection regulations. Organizations must implement strong security practices and ensure that cloud providers meet their data security and privacy requirements.

Vendor lock-in is another challenge associated with cloud adoption. Once an organization heavily invests in a specific cloud provider's services and tools, transitioning to another provider or returning to an on-premises environment can be complex and costly. Organizations should consider multi-cloud strategies to mitigate vendor lock-in risks.

Cost management and optimization are ongoing challenges in cloud adoption. While the pay-as-you-go model can lead to cost savings, it can also result in unexpected expenses if resources are not monitored and optimized continuously. Implementing cost monitoring and management tools is crucial to control cloud spending effectively.

Performance and latency can be concerns, especially for applications that require low latency or high-performance computing. Organizations need to assess the performance characteristics of cloud services and select the appropriate instance types and configurations to meet their application requirements.

Furthermore, compliance and regulatory considerations can be challenging in the cloud. Organizations operating in regulated industries must ensure that their cloud environment complies with industry-specific regulations and standards. Cloud providers may offer compliance certifications and audit reports to assist with these requirements.

Data transfer costs can also be a significant expense in cloud adoption, especially for organizations with large data volumes. Understanding data transfer pricing and optimizing data transfer patterns can help mitigate these costs.

Lastly, the complexity of managing a multi-cloud or hybrid cloud environment can introduce operational challenges. Organizations need to establish effective governance, monitoring, and management practices to ensure the seamless operation of their cloud infrastructure.

In summary, cloud adoption offers numerous benefits, including flexibility, cost savings, agility, and enhanced collaboration and security. However, it also presents challenges related to data security, vendor lock-in, cost management, performance, compliance, data transfer costs, and operational complexity. To maximize the benefits of cloud adoption while mitigating these challenges, organizations must carefully plan their cloud strategy, implement robust security measures, continuously monitor and optimize their cloud environment, and stay informed about emerging best practices and technologies in cloud computing.

## Chapter 2: Cloud Service Providers and Platforms

Major cloud service providers, also known as cloud providers or hyperscale cloud providers, are companies that offer a wide range of cloud computing services and resources to organizations and individuals. These providers have built massive data centers and infrastructure that enable customers to access and utilize cloud services on a global scale.

Amazon Web Services (AWS) is one of the most prominent cloud service providers, offering a comprehensive suite of cloud services that include computing power, storage, databases, machine learning, analytics, and more. AWS is known for its extensive global network of data centers, which allows customers to deploy applications and services in multiple regions around the world.

Microsoft Azure, another major player in the cloud industry, provides a wide array of cloud services, including virtual machines, databases, AI and machine learning tools, and Internet of Things (IoT) solutions. Azure is highly regarded for its integration with Microsoft's software products and services, making it a popular choice for organizations already using Microsoft technologies.

Google Cloud Platform (GCP) is known for its strengths in data analytics, machine learning, and artificial intelligence. GCP offers a variety of cloud services, including computing, storage, databases, and Kubernetes-based container orchestration. Google's extensive expertise in data handling and analysis attracts organizations seeking advanced analytics capabilities.

IBM Cloud caters to both enterprises and smaller businesses, offering cloud infrastructure, cloud-native development tools, and services like artificial intelligence and blockchain. IBM's long history in enterprise technology makes it a trusted provider for organizations with specific enterprise-grade requirements.

Oracle Cloud is a cloud platform designed for businesses that rely on Oracle's software and databases. It offers cloud infrastructure, database services, applications, and autonomous computing. Oracle Cloud is a popular choice for organizations looking to migrate their Oracle workloads to the cloud.

Alibaba Cloud, the cloud division of Alibaba Group, is a leading provider of cloud services in Asia and globally. Alibaba Cloud offers a broad range of cloud computing and data storage services, catering to organizations looking to expand their presence in the Asian market.

Salesforce, primarily known for its customer relationship management (CRM) software, also provides cloud services through Salesforce Cloud. The company offers a platform-as-a-service (PaaS) solution called Salesforce Platform, allowing businesses to build and deploy custom applications.

Tencent Cloud, a subsidiary of Tencent Holdings, is a major player in the Asian cloud market. It provides cloud computing, data storage, and artificial intelligence services, making it a popular choice for organizations operating in the Asia-Pacific region.

DigitalOcean focuses on simplicity and ease of use, offering cloud services tailored to developers and startups. DigitalOcean's services include virtual private servers (known as Droplets), managed databases, and Kubernetes-based container orchestration.

Rackspace Technology, while not a traditional cloud provider, offers managed cloud services and multi-cloud solutions, helping organizations optimize and manage their cloud environments across various cloud providers.

Oracle Cloud is a cloud platform designed for businesses that rely on Oracle's software and databases. It offers cloud infrastructure, database services, applications, and autonomous computing. Oracle Cloud is a popular choice for organizations looking to migrate their Oracle workloads to the cloud.

Alibaba Cloud, the cloud division of Alibaba Group, is a leading provider of cloud services in Asia and globally. Alibaba Cloud offers a broad range of cloud computing and data storage services, catering to organizations looking to expand their presence in the Asian market.

Salesforce, primarily known for its customer relationship management (CRM) software, also provides cloud services through Salesforce Cloud. The company offers a platform-as-a-service (PaaS) solution called Salesforce Platform, allowing businesses to build and deploy custom applications.

Tencent Cloud, a subsidiary of Tencent Holdings, is a major player in the Asian cloud market. It provides cloud computing, data storage, and artificial intelligence services, making it a popular choice for organizations operating in the Asia-Pacific region.

DigitalOcean focuses on simplicity and ease of use, offering cloud services tailored to developers and startups. DigitalOcean's services include virtual private servers (known as Droplets), managed databases, and Kubernetes-based container orchestration.

Rackspace Technology, while not a traditional cloud provider, offers managed cloud services and multi-cloud solutions, helping organizations optimize and manage their cloud environments across various cloud providers.

Each of these major cloud service providers offers unique strengths and capabilities, making them suitable for different use cases and business requirements. Organizations evaluating cloud providers must consider factors such as service offerings, pricing models, compliance requirements, and geographic presence when selecting the right provider for their needs. Additionally, many organizations adopt a multi-cloud or hybrid cloud strategy, leveraging multiple cloud providers to gain the benefits of diversity, redundancy, and specialized services.

Selecting the right cloud platform is a critical decision for organizations embarking on their cloud journey, as it can significantly impact their ability to achieve their business goals and meet their technological needs. The choice of a cloud platform involves evaluating various factors, understanding the specific requirements of the organization, and aligning those needs with the capabilities of the cloud providers.

First and foremost, organizations should assess their existing IT infrastructure, applications, and data to determine what can be migrated or modernized in the cloud. This assessment helps in understanding the scope and scale of the cloud adoption project and provides insights into which cloud services and resources will be required.

It is essential to define clear objectives and goals for moving to the cloud, whether it's cost reduction, scalability, agility, innovation, or a combination of these factors. These objectives will serve as a guide when evaluating cloud providers and their offerings.

Understanding the different types of cloud services is crucial. Infrastructure as a Service (IaaS) provides virtualized computing resources, Platform as a Service (PaaS) offers a platform for application development, and Software as a Service (SaaS) delivers fully functional applications over the internet. Organizations must decide which service models align with their needs.

The choice between public, private, or hybrid cloud deployment models depends on factors like data sensitivity, compliance requirements, and the need for customization. Public clouds are hosted and managed by third-party providers, private clouds are dedicated to a single organization, and hybrid clouds combine elements of both.

Consider the geographic presence of the cloud provider's data centers and regions. Organizations with a global footprint may require a provider with a wide network of data centers to ensure low-latency access and data sovereignty compliance.

Evaluating the cloud provider's ecosystem and marketplace is essential. A rich ecosystem provides a variety of third-party integrations, tools, and services that can enhance an organization's cloud environment and support specific business needs.

Service-level agreements (SLAs) define the terms of service availability, performance, and support.

Organizations should review SLAs carefully to ensure they align with their requirements and expectations.

Security is a paramount concern when choosing a cloud platform. Cloud providers invest heavily in security measures, but organizations are responsible for securing their data and applications in the cloud. Ensure that the provider offers robust security features and compliance certifications.

Cost considerations are significant in cloud adoption. Organizations should have a clear understanding of pricing models, such as pay-as-you-go, reserved instances, or subscription plans, and calculate potential costs based on their usage patterns.

Vendor lock-in is a concern when relying heavily on a specific cloud provider's proprietary services and tools. To mitigate this risk, organizations may adopt a multi-cloud or hybrid cloud strategy to maintain flexibility and reduce dependency.

Understanding the provider's support and customer service offerings is essential. Evaluate the availability of support channels, response times, and access to technical expertise when needed.

Organizations should also consider the provider's track record and reputation in terms of reliability, uptime, and customer satisfaction. Customer reviews and industry reports can provide insights into the provider's performance.

Scalability and flexibility are core cloud benefits. The chosen cloud platform should support the organization's growth and evolving needs without requiring significant redesign or migration efforts.

A robust cloud management and monitoring toolset is crucial for efficiently managing cloud resources, optimizing costs, and ensuring compliance with policies.

Organizations should also assess the provider's commitment to sustainability and environmental responsibility, as these factors may align with their corporate values and goals.

Finally, conducting a proof of concept or a pilot project on the selected cloud platform can provide hands-on experience and validate that the chosen solution meets the organization's needs and expectations.

In summary, choosing the right cloud platform is a complex and strategic decision that requires a comprehensive assessment of the organization's requirements, objectives, and constraints. It involves evaluating factors such as service models, deployment models, security, cost, support, scalability, and more. By thoroughly researching and considering these factors, organizations can make an informed decision that aligns with their business goals and sets the stage for a successful cloud adoption journey.

## Chapter 3: Deploying Virtual Machines in the Cloud

Creating virtual machines (VMs) is a fundamental process in cloud computing and virtualization, allowing organizations to run multiple operating systems and applications on a single physical server. VMs offer flexibility, scalability, and isolation, making them a valuable resource for various use cases.

The process of creating a VM typically begins with selecting a virtualization platform or cloud provider that supports VM deployment, such as VMware, Hyper-V, KVM, VirtualBox, or a public cloud platform like Amazon Web Services (AWS), Microsoft Azure, or Google Cloud Platform (GCP).

Once the platform is chosen, the next step is to define the specifications of the VM, including the amount of CPU, memory, storage, and network resources it will have access to. These specifications determine the VM's performance and capabilities.

The choice of the guest operating system is crucial, as it determines the software and applications that can run on the VM. Common guest operating systems include various versions of Windows, Linux distributions, and specialized OSes for specific applications or purposes.

To create a VM, administrators or users typically use a virtualization management tool or the cloud provider's web-based console. These tools offer a user-friendly interface for configuring VM settings and initiating the creation process.

During the VM creation process, users can define parameters such as the VM's name, location, and resource allocation. They can also specify the installation method for the guest operating system, which may involve using an ISO image, network-based installation, or cloning an existing VM template.

Network configuration is an essential step in VM creation, as it determines how the VM connects to the network and the internet. Users can assign IP addresses, configure DNS settings, and set up virtual network interfaces to establish connectivity.

Storage options for VMs include choosing the type of virtual hard disk (VHD) or virtual machine disk (VMDK) format, selecting the storage location, and specifying the size of the VM's disk. Some virtualization platforms also offer features like thin provisioning to optimize disk usage.

Once the VM's configuration is defined, users initiate the creation process, which typically involves provisioning the necessary resources on the physical host server, such as CPU cores, memory, and disk space.

The VM creation process also involves copying the selected guest operating system image or template to the VM's storage location. This step is critical for the VM's initial boot and installation.

After the VM is provisioned and the guest OS is installed, users can further customize the VM by installing additional software, configuring system settings, and applying security updates.

Many virtualization platforms and cloud providers offer features for VM management and automation, such as snapshots, cloning, and templates. Snapshots allow users to capture a point-in-time image of the VM's state, which can be useful for backup, recovery, or testing purposes.

Cloning enables users to create identical copies of existing VMs, simplifying the deployment of multiple VMs with similar configurations. Templates are preconfigured VM images that can serve as a starting point for new VMs, streamlining the provisioning process.

VM management tools also provide monitoring and performance optimization features, allowing users to track resource utilization, detect performance bottlenecks, and make adjustments as needed.

Security is a critical consideration when creating VMs, and organizations should implement best practices for securing both the host server and the VMs themselves. This includes applying security patches, using firewalls, implementing access controls, and regularly auditing VM configurations.

Backup and disaster recovery strategies are essential for VMs, as they ensure data protection and business continuity. Organizations should implement backup solutions that regularly capture VM snapshots and store them in secure locations.

Testing and validation are crucial aspects of VM creation, as they help ensure that the VM operates as intended and meets the organization's requirements. Users should thoroughly test VMs before deploying them in production environments to identify and resolve any issues.

In summary, creating virtual machines is a fundamental process in cloud computing and virtualization, enabling organizations to leverage the benefits of flexibility, scalability, and isolation. The process involves selecting a virtualization platform, defining VM specifications, configuring guest operating systems, network settings, and storage options, and using management tools for provisioning, customization, and ongoing management. Security, backup, and testing are essential considerations to ensure the reliable and secure operation of VMs in various use cases and environments.

Configuring cloud virtual machines (VMs) for optimal performance and security is a critical aspect of cloud infrastructure management, as it directly impacts the reliability and stability of applications and services hosted in the cloud environment. Achieving the right balance between performance and security is a nuanced task that requires careful consideration of various factors.

Performance optimization starts with selecting the appropriate VM instance type based on the specific workload and resource requirements. Different cloud providers offer a range of instance types, each with varying amounts of CPU, memory, and storage. Understanding the workload's characteristics and resource demands is crucial for making the right choice.

In addition to instance type selection, optimizing VM performance involves fine-tuning various parameters within the VM's operating system and application stack. This may include adjusting kernel parameters, optimizing disk I/O, and configuring network settings to reduce latency and improve throughput.

Scaling strategies, such as vertical scaling (resizing the VM to a higher instance type) and horizontal scaling (adding more VM instances), can be employed to accommodate fluctuating workloads. Autoscaling, a cloud service feature, automates the process of adjusting the number of VM instances based on predefined criteria.

To further enhance performance, organizations can leverage content delivery networks (CDNs) and edge computing. CDNs cache and deliver content closer to end-users, reducing latency and improving the user experience. Edge computing places computing resources closer to the data source, enabling real-time processing for applications like IoT and content delivery.

Security considerations are paramount when configuring cloud VMs. It's essential to implement robust security measures to protect against threats and vulnerabilities. One fundamental practice is to keep the VM's operating system and software up to date with security patches and updates.

Access control and authentication mechanisms must be configured to ensure that only authorized users and systems can interact with the VM. Identity and access management (IAM) tools provided by cloud providers enable fine-grained control over user permissions and roles.

Firewalls and network security groups (NSGs) can be used to restrict inbound and outbound traffic to and from the VM. By defining rules based on IP addresses and port ranges, organizations can create a secure network perimeter around the VM.

Encryption is a critical security measure for protecting data both at rest and in transit. Cloud providers offer encryption options for data storage, and organizations can implement secure communication protocols (e.g., HTTPS, SSH) to encrypt data in transit.

Vulnerability assessments and security scanning tools help organizations identify and address security weaknesses in their VM configurations and applications. Regular security audits and compliance checks are essential to maintain a strong security posture.

Data backups and disaster recovery plans are integral components of VM security. Organizations should regularly back up VM data and configurations to ensure data integrity and rapid recovery in the event of data loss or system failures.

Intrusion detection and prevention systems (IDS/IPS) can be deployed to monitor and safeguard VMs against malicious activities. These systems can identify and block suspicious network traffic and system behavior.

Additionally, organizations should follow security best practices such as the principle of least privilege, which limits user and system permissions to the minimum necessary for their tasks. This minimizes the potential impact of security breaches.

Logging and auditing are essential for security monitoring and compliance. VMs should generate and store logs that capture relevant security events and system activities. Automated log analysis tools can help detect anomalies and security incidents.

To protect against distributed denial-of-service (DDoS) attacks, organizations can use DDoS protection services provided by cloud providers. These services can absorb and mitigate DDoS traffic to ensure uninterrupted service availability.

Compliance with industry-specific regulations and standards is crucial for organizations in regulated sectors, such as healthcare and finance. Cloud providers offer compliance certifications and audit reports to demonstrate adherence to these requirements.

Lastly, organizations should create an incident response plan that outlines the steps to take in the event of a security breach or incident. This plan should include communication protocols, mitigation strategies, and recovery procedures.

In summary, configuring cloud VMs for performance and security is a multifaceted task that requires careful consideration of resource allocation, scaling strategies, security measures, and compliance requirements. Balancing performance and security is a continuous process that involves ongoing monitoring, optimization, and adaptation to evolving threats and workloads. By following best practices and leveraging cloud provider services and tools, organizations can create a secure and high-performing cloud VM environment that supports their business objectives and safeguards their data and applications.

# Chapter 4: Infrastructure as Code (IaC) Principles

Infrastructure as Code (IaC) is a fundamental concept in modern cloud computing and DevOps practices, enabling organizations to manage and provision their infrastructure through code rather than manual processes.

At its core, IaC treats infrastructure components such as virtual machines, networks, and storage as code artifacts, which are defined using human-readable code files.

These code files are typically written in domain-specific languages or configuration files and are used to declare the desired state of the infrastructure.

One of the primary benefits of IaC is that it brings automation to infrastructure provisioning and management, reducing the need for manual interventions and minimizing human errors.

IaC enables infrastructure to be version-controlled, allowing organizations to track changes, collaborate among team members, and roll back to previous configurations if issues arise.

By representing infrastructure as code, organizations can achieve greater consistency and repeatability in their deployments, ensuring that each environment is identical and eliminating the "it works on my machine" problem.

IaC encourages a declarative approach, where users specify what they want their infrastructure to look like rather than providing step-by-step instructions on how to achieve that state.

This declarative approach abstracts the underlying complexity of infrastructure provisioning, making it more accessible to a wider range of users, including developers and system administrators.

In contrast to manual provisioning, where each change must be made individually, IaC allows users to define the desired state and rely on automation tools to bring the infrastructure into that state.

This automation can be achieved through various IaC tools and frameworks, such as Terraform, AWS CloudFormation, Ansible, Puppet, and Chef, each offering its unique capabilities and syntax.

Terraform, for example, uses HashiCorp Configuration Language (HCL) to define infrastructure as code, while AWS CloudFormation relies on JSON or YAML templates.

IaC tools typically support a wide range of cloud providers and services, allowing organizations to manage infrastructure across multiple platforms through a single set of code files.

With IaC, infrastructure changes can be reviewed, tested, and validated through automated pipelines, ensuring that new configurations are stable and compliant before being applied to production environments.

Furthermore, IaC promotes collaboration between development and operations teams, fostering a DevOps culture where both groups work together to achieve a common goal.

When implementing IaC, organizations can take advantage of version control systems, such as Git, to manage their code repositories and track changes over time.

Version control not only helps with change management but also provides an audit trail for all modifications to infrastructure code.

Additionally, IaC code can be stored in centralized repositories or shared across teams, enabling collaboration, code reuse, and best practice sharing.

One of the essential principles of IaC is idempotence, which means that applying the same configuration multiple times will have the same result as applying it once.

This ensures that infrastructure code can be safely applied, even in situations where it needs to be executed multiple times or during system failures.

In the context of IaC, idempotence is achieved by designing code in a way that checks the current state of the infrastructure and only makes necessary changes to bring it to the desired state.

It is important to note that IaC is not limited to the provisioning of infrastructure resources but also encompasses the configuration of software and applications running on that infrastructure.

By defining both the infrastructure and application configurations as code, organizations can achieve end-to-end automation and consistency in their deployments.

IaC can be applied to various use cases, from setting up development and testing environments to deploying production systems and managing cloud-native architectures.

In summary, Infrastructure as Code (IaC) is a transformative concept in cloud computing and DevOps, allowing organizations to manage and provision infrastructure through code files.

IaC promotes automation, consistency, and collaboration, abstracting the complexity of infrastructure provisioning and enabling teams to work together to achieve a common goal.

By representing infrastructure and application configurations as code, organizations can achieve end-to-end automation and ensure that their deployments are stable, reliable, and idempotent.

IaC is supported by a variety of tools and frameworks, each with its unique syntax and capabilities, making it accessible and adaptable to different cloud providers and services.

Overall, IaC is a fundamental practice for modern cloud-native and DevOps-driven organizations, enabling them to accelerate their deployment processes, minimize errors, and achieve greater agility and reliability in their infrastructure management.

Infrastructure as Code (IaC) is a transformative approach to managing and provisioning infrastructure through code, and it has gained widespread adoption in the world of cloud computing and DevOps.

To implement IaC effectively, organizations rely on a variety of IaC tools and practices that enable them to automate infrastructure tasks and maintain consistency across environments.

One of the key IaC practices is the use of version control systems like Git to store and manage infrastructure code.

Version control allows teams to collaborate on infrastructure code, track changes, and roll back to previous configurations if needed.

By treating infrastructure code like any other software code, organizations can benefit from code reviews, branching strategies, and a history of changes, enhancing collaboration and change management.

Another crucial practice is the use of templates or configuration files to define infrastructure resources and their desired state.

These templates, often written in domain-specific languages or declarative syntax, serve as blueprints for provisioning resources such as virtual machines, networks, and storage.

IaC templates are typically stored in code repositories, ensuring versioning, traceability, and code reuse.

Popular IaC tools like Terraform, AWS CloudFormation, Ansible, Puppet, and Chef provide frameworks for defining infrastructure as code.

Terraform, for instance, uses HashiCorp Configuration Language (HCL) to describe infrastructure resources, while AWS CloudFormation relies on JSON or YAML templates.

Declarative templates specify what the infrastructure should look like, and IaC tools handle the provisioning and management of resources to achieve that state.

In addition to defining infrastructure, IaC practices also encompass the orchestration of changes to infrastructure resources.

This includes creating, updating, and deleting resources based on changes made to the IaC code.

IaC tools provide mechanisms for applying changes in a controlled and automated manner, ensuring that the infrastructure remains in the desired state.

Infrastructure changes can be tracked and tested in development and staging environments before being applied to production, reducing the risk of errors and downtime.

Continuous integration and continuous delivery (CI/CD) pipelines play a vital role in IaC practices, allowing organizations to automate the testing and deployment of infrastructure code changes.

CI/CD pipelines integrate with version control systems to trigger automated tests, code validation, and deployment of infrastructure changes.

By incorporating infrastructure code into CI/CD pipelines, organizations can ensure that changes are thoroughly tested and validated before reaching production environments.

An essential aspect of IaC is idempotence, which ensures that applying the same infrastructure code multiple times results in the same state as applying it once.

Idempotence is achieved by designing IaC code to check the current state of the infrastructure and make changes only if necessary.

This property is critical for safely applying infrastructure code in various scenarios, such as system failures or reapplying code during recovery.

Another practice in IaC is the separation of configuration from secrets and sensitive data.

Sensitive information, such as passwords and API keys, should not be hard-coded in infrastructure code but should instead be managed securely through secrets management tools and services.

This separation enhances security and minimizes the risk of exposing sensitive data in code repositories.

Collaboration and role-based access control are crucial IaC practices for ensuring that teams can work together efficiently and securely.

Role-based access control defines who can perform specific actions and make changes to infrastructure code and resources.

This practice enforces the principle of least privilege, limiting user access to only what is necessary for their roles and responsibilities.

Regular auditing and monitoring of infrastructure changes are essential IaC practices to maintain visibility and compliance.

Organizations should implement monitoring and logging solutions that capture infrastructure events and activities.

Auditing infrastructure changes helps identify anomalies, enforce compliance policies, and provide an audit trail for security and compliance purposes. Another IaC practice is the use of modularization and reusable code components.

Organizations can create reusable modules or templates that define common infrastructure patterns and configurations.

These modules can be shared across teams and projects, promoting consistency and reducing duplication of effort.

IaC practices also include the use of testing frameworks and automated testing procedures for infrastructure code.

Unit tests, integration tests, and validation tests can help ensure that infrastructure code functions as intended and meets predefined criteria.

Automated testing provides confidence in the stability and correctness of infrastructure changes.

Documentation is a fundamental IaC practice to ensure that infrastructure code is well-documented, including explanations of resource configurations, dependencies, and usage guidelines.

Clear and up-to-date documentation facilitates collaboration, troubleshooting, and knowledge sharing among team members.

Lastly, continuous improvement is an ongoing IaC practice that encourages organizations to evaluate and refine their infrastructure code and practices.

Feedback from users, monitoring data, and post-implementation reviews can inform changes and enhancements to the IaC process.

In summary, Infrastructure as Code (IaC) is supported by a set of essential tools and practices that enable organizations to manage and provision infrastructure through code.

These practices encompass version control, templates, orchestration, continuous integration and delivery (CI/CD), idempotence, secrets management, collaboration, auditing, modularization, testing, documentation, and continuous improvement.

By adopting these IaC practices, organizations can automate infrastructure tasks, maintain consistency, improve collaboration, enhance security, and achieve greater agility in their cloud and DevOps initiatives.

## Chapter 5: Managing Cloud Resources with Terraform

Getting started with Terraform is an exciting journey into the world of Infrastructure as Code (IaC) and cloud automation, and it opens up a realm of possibilities for managing and provisioning infrastructure in a more efficient and scalable way.

Terraform is an open-source IaC tool developed by HashiCorp that allows you to define, provision, and manage infrastructure resources through declarative code, which means you describe what you want the infrastructure to look like, and Terraform takes care of making it happen.

To begin your Terraform journey, you'll first need to install Terraform on your local development environment, and it's essential to use a version that is compatible with the cloud providers and services you plan to work with.

Terraform is available for various operating systems, including Windows, macOS, and Linux, and installation instructions can be found on the official Terraform website or package manager of your choice.

Once Terraform is installed, the next step is to choose your cloud provider or infrastructure platform, such as Amazon Web Services (AWS), Microsoft Azure, Google Cloud Platform (GCP), or even on-premises solutions like VMware vSphere.

Terraform supports a wide range of providers, enabling you to manage infrastructure resources across different cloud providers and services, or even combine resources from multiple providers within a single configuration.

With Terraform, infrastructure configurations are defined using HashiCorp Configuration Language (HCL), a domain-specific language designed for writing IaC code.

HCL is human-readable and easy to understand, making it accessible to both developers and operators who want to collaborate on defining and managing infrastructure.

Terraform configurations typically reside in files with a .tf extension, and you can organize your configurations into modules for better modularity and reusability.

Before you start writing your Terraform configurations, it's essential to plan and design your infrastructure, outlining the resources you need and their dependencies.

This planning phase helps you create a clear vision of your infrastructure's architecture and ensures that your Terraform code accurately reflects your intentions.

To configure Terraform for a specific cloud provider, you need to define a provider block in your configuration, specifying details like the provider name, access credentials, and region.

For example, if you're working with AWS, you'd define a provider block with your AWS access key and secret key, specifying the desired AWS region.

Terraform uses this information to authenticate and interact with your chosen provider's API.

Once the provider is configured, you can start defining the infrastructure resources you want to create, such as virtual machines, networks, storage, and security groups.

Resources are declared using resource blocks in your Terraform configuration files, with each resource block specifying the resource type and its associated attributes.

Attributes are used to provide additional information and configuration details for each resource, such as the size of a virtual machine or the name of a network.

Terraform supports a wide variety of resource types, and you can find detailed documentation for each provider on the Terraform website.

One of the key features of Terraform is its ability to manage resource dependencies and ensure that resources are created and configured in the correct order.

Terraform automatically determines the order in which resources should be provisioned based on their dependencies, simplifying the provisioning process and minimizing errors.

As you define your resources, you can use Terraform's interpolation syntax to reference attributes from one resource within another.

This allows you to pass information between resources and create dynamic configurations.

Terraform also provides the concept of variables, which enable you to parameterize your configurations and make them more flexible.

Variables allow you to define placeholders in your configurations that can be set externally when you apply your Terraform code, making it easy to reuse configurations with different input values.

In addition to variables, Terraform supports data sources, which allow you to query information from your cloud provider or other external sources and use that data within your configurations.

For example, you can use a data source to retrieve information about an existing virtual network and use that information to configure a new virtual machine.

After defining your infrastructure resources, you can use Terraform commands to validate your configuration and plan the changes that will be made to your infrastructure.

The terraform init command initializes your Terraform project, downloading any necessary plugins and modules.

The terraform validate command checks your configuration for syntax errors and other issues.

The terraform plan command generates an execution plan that shows what actions Terraform will take when you apply your configuration.

Reviewing the execution plan is a critical step to ensure that your configurations align with your expectations.

To apply your Terraform configuration and create or modify resources, you can use the terraform apply command.

Terraform will prompt you to confirm the changes before proceeding to make the modifications.

Once the apply is complete, Terraform stores the state of your infrastructure in a state file, which is used to track the current state of your resources.

The state file is crucial for Terraform to understand the existing state of your infrastructure and determine how to make changes in subsequent runs.

It's essential to keep the state file secure and version-controlled to ensure consistency and maintainability of your infrastructure.

As you continue to work with Terraform, you'll likely encounter the need to manage variables and secrets securely.

Terraform provides mechanisms for managing sensitive information, such as variable input files and environment variables, to ensure that sensitive data is protected and not exposed in your configurations.

Additionally, Terraform offers a remote state management feature, which allows you to store the state file in a central and secure location, making it easier to collaborate with team members and manage the state across multiple environments.

Terraform's ecosystem includes a rich library of modules and plugins created by the community and supported by HashiCorp.

Modules are reusable configurations that encapsulate infrastructure components and can be shared and reused across projects.

Using modules can significantly accelerate your infrastructure development and promote best practices in configuration design.

In summary, getting started with Terraform involves installing the tool, selecting your cloud provider or infrastructure platform, planning and designing your infrastructure, writing Terraform configurations using HCL, and using Terraform commands to validate, plan, and apply your configurations.

Terraform provides powerful features for managing infrastructure as code, including resource dependencies, variables, data sources, and remote state management.

With Terraform, you can automate your infrastructure provisioning, improve consistency, and embrace the principles of Infrastructure as Code to achieve greater efficiency and agility in your cloud and DevOps workflows.

Creating and managing infrastructure with Terraform is a powerful and flexible approach that empowers organizations to automate the provisioning and maintenance of cloud resources and on-premises infrastructure.

Terraform, developed by HashiCorp, is an Infrastructure as Code (IaC) tool that enables users to define their desired infrastructure configurations as code, making it easier to deploy and manage infrastructure at scale.

The process of creating and managing infrastructure with Terraform begins by defining infrastructure resources and their configurations in Terraform files using HashiCorp Configuration Language (HCL).

These Terraform files describe the desired state of the infrastructure, such as virtual machines, networks, databases, and security policies, and provide details on how these resources should be provisioned and configured.

Infrastructure resources are defined using resource blocks, which specify the resource type and its attributes within the Terraform file.

Attributes within resource blocks include information like resource names, sizes, regions, and dependencies, allowing users to precisely tailor their infrastructure to their needs.

Terraform's strength lies in its ability to support various cloud providers, including Amazon Web Services (AWS), Microsoft Azure, Google Cloud Platform (GCP), and others. This cross-provider compatibility allows organizations to use a single set of Terraform configurations to manage infrastructure resources across different cloud environments, reducing complexity and streamlining operations.

Once infrastructure configurations are defined, the next step is to initialize the Terraform project using the "terraform init" command.

This command downloads the necessary plugins and modules required to interact with the chosen cloud provider's API and execute the Terraform configurations.

Initialization sets up the project, ensuring that it's ready to validate, plan, and apply infrastructure changes.

After initialization, the "terraform validate" command can be used to check the Terraform configurations for errors and validate their syntax.

Validation is a critical step to identify any issues within the Terraform files before attempting to apply them to the infrastructure.

Upon successful validation, the "terraform plan" command generates an execution plan that outlines the actions Terraform will take to bring the infrastructure into the desired state.

The execution plan provides users with insights into the changes that will occur, including the creation, modification, or deletion of resources.

Reviewing the plan is crucial to ensure that the proposed changes align with the organization's intentions and expectations.

Terraform's declarative approach to infrastructure management means that users specify the desired end-state, and Terraform takes care of determining how to achieve that state, including creating or modifying resources in the correct order.

To apply the Terraform configurations and enact the changes outlined in the execution plan, users run the "terraform apply" command.

Terraform will prompt users to confirm the changes, allowing for a final review before proceeding with the execution.

Applying the configurations initiates the provisioning and modification of infrastructure resources based on the defined specifications.

During this process, Terraform communicates with the cloud provider's APIs to create, update, or delete resources, ensuring that the infrastructure aligns with the specified state.

Once the "terraform apply" process is complete, Terraform stores the current state of the infrastructure in a state file.

This state file is essential for Terraform to understand the existing state of resources and track changes over time.

It also prevents Terraform from creating duplicate resources or making unnecessary modifications when subsequent changes are applied.

Managing the Terraform state file is a critical consideration, and organizations should adopt practices that ensure its security and accessibility.

To maintain an organized and efficient Terraform project, users can modularize their configurations into reusable modules.

Modules encapsulate specific infrastructure components or patterns, allowing users to create a library of reusable building blocks.

Using modules promotes code reuse, standardization, and consistency, making it easier to manage complex infrastructure configurations across different projects and teams.

Terraform modules can be shared within an organization or even published to the Terraform Registry for broader community use.

Managing infrastructure with Terraform also involves handling variables, which allow users to parameterize their configurations and make them more adaptable.

Variables serve as placeholders in the Terraform files and can be defined in separate variable files or specified as command-line arguments during the "terraform apply" process.

Using variables makes it possible to customize configurations for different environments, regions, or purposes, while still adhering to the same Terraform codebase.

Sensitive information, such as API keys, passwords, and access tokens, should be managed securely when working with Terraform configurations.

Terraform provides mechanisms for handling secrets, such as environment variables and remote state storage with encryption.

Organizations should implement secure practices for managing secrets to prevent exposure and unauthorized access.

Infrastructure as Code (IaC) practices extend to managing the entire lifecycle of infrastructure resources, including scaling, updating, and destroying resources.

Terraform's "terraform plan" and "terraform apply" commands can be used iteratively to manage changes to existing infrastructure.

Updating resources is as simple as modifying the Terraform configurations and reapplying them using "terraform apply."

Terraform will analyze the changes and apply only the necessary modifications to bring the infrastructure to the desired state.

When it's time to scale infrastructure, whether adding more virtual machines or increasing storage capacity, Terraform configurations can be updated to reflect the new requirements.

Terraform's ability to manage resource dependencies ensures that scaling operations are performed in a controlled and consistent manner.

When infrastructure resources are no longer needed, Terraform allows users to destroy them by running the "terraform destroy" command.

This command dismantles resources, releases associated cloud resources, and updates the Terraform state file to reflect the removal.

It's essential to exercise caution when using "terraform destroy" to prevent unintentional resource deletion.

In summary, creating and managing infrastructure with Terraform involves defining infrastructure configurations as code, initializing the Terraform project, validating configurations, generating execution plans, applying changes, and tracking the state of resources.

Terraform supports a wide range of cloud providers and enables cross-provider compatibility, making it a versatile choice for managing infrastructure across different environments.

By adopting Infrastructure as Code practices with Terraform, organizations can achieve greater automation, consistency, and scalability in their infrastructure management, while also promoting collaboration and code reuse.

## Chapter 6: Automating Deployments with Ansible

Ansible is a powerful open-source automation tool that simplifies the management and configuration of servers, applications, and infrastructure in a scalable and efficient manner.

It is designed to automate repetitive tasks, streamline complex workflows, and enable infrastructure as code (IaC) practices.

Ansible's simplicity, flexibility, and agentless architecture make it a popular choice for IT professionals and DevOps teams seeking to improve the efficiency and reliability of their operations.

At its core, Ansible is a configuration management tool that allows you to define the desired state of your infrastructure and automate the process of bringing it into that state.

With Ansible, you express your infrastructure configurations in simple, human-readable YAML files known as playbooks.

These playbooks describe the tasks to be performed and the target hosts on which these tasks should execute.

Ansible then takes care of executing these tasks on the target hosts and ensures that the desired state is achieved.

One of Ansible's standout features is its agentless architecture, which eliminates the need to install and manage agents or clients on target hosts.

Instead, Ansible uses SSH or WinRM (on Windows systems) to securely connect to remote hosts and execute tasks through a simple and secure communication protocol.

This agentless approach simplifies the setup and maintenance of managed hosts and reduces potential security risks associated with agent-based solutions.

Ansible playbooks consist of a series of tasks that define the actions to be taken on target hosts.

Tasks can range from installing software packages, configuring system settings, copying files, starting services, and more.

Each task is associated with a module, which is a small, standalone program responsible for executing a specific action on the target host.

Ansible provides a wide range of built-in modules for common tasks, and you can also create custom modules to meet specific needs.

Variables play a significant role in Ansible, allowing you to parameterize your playbooks and make them more flexible and reusable.

You can define variables at various levels, including playbook-level, role-level, and host-level, and use them to customize task behavior.

This flexibility makes it possible to deploy the same playbook with different configurations to multiple hosts or environments.

Ansible provides several ways to organize and structure your automation code, including roles, which are reusable collections of tasks, templates, and variables.

Roles help modularize your playbooks, making them more maintainable and promoting code reuse across projects.

Roles can be shared within your organization or with the wider Ansible community through Ansible Galaxy, a repository of Ansible roles contributed by the community.

In addition to configuration management, Ansible excels at orchestration, allowing you to define complex workflows and coordinate actions across multiple hosts and services.

You can use Ansible to automate multi-step processes, such as application deployments, database migrations, and disaster recovery procedures.

Ansible's idempotent nature ensures that running the same playbook multiple times has the same result as running it once, making it safe to use for ongoing automation and configuration management.

Inventory management is another essential aspect of Ansible, as it defines the list of hosts and groups of hosts that Ansible will manage.

You can configure your inventory manually in INI-style files or dynamically generate it from external sources like cloud providers or LDAP directories.

This dynamic inventory feature allows Ansible to adapt to changing infrastructure environments and automatically discover and manage hosts.

Playbooks can be executed against inventory groups, making it easy to target specific sets of hosts with common configurations or tasks.

Ansible includes a powerful feature called roles, which are reusable collections of tasks, variables, and templates that can be organized into structured directories.

Roles promote modularity, code reuse, and maintainability in Ansible automation.

You can use roles to encapsulate specific functionality, such as setting up a web server or configuring a database, and then include these roles in your playbooks.

This modular approach allows you to build complex automation by composing roles and focusing on specific aspects of your infrastructure.

Ansible also supports the use of Jinja2 templates within playbooks and roles, enabling you to generate configuration files dynamically based on variables and conditions.

This template-driven approach allows for flexible and customizable configuration generation while maintaining the simplicity and readability of your automation code.

Error handling and reporting are integral to Ansible's design, ensuring that you can handle exceptions gracefully and gain insights into the success or failure of playbook runs.

You can define error handling strategies, retry failed tasks, and specify custom failure handlers to take specific actions when errors occur.

Ansible provides detailed logs and reports to help you troubleshoot issues and track the execution of your automation tasks.

Ansible includes a vast collection of pre-built modules that cover a wide range of tasks, from basic system administration to cloud orchestration and application deployment.

These modules are continually updated and expanded by the Ansible community, making it easier to automate various aspects of your infrastructure.

Ansible also supports a wide range of platforms and operating systems, including Linux, Windows, macOS, and various cloud providers such as AWS, Azure, and Google Cloud.

This cross-platform support allows you to use Ansible for managing diverse environments and heterogeneous infrastructures.

Ansible provides a powerful inventory system that allows you to define and organize the hosts you want to manage.

You can create host groups, assign variables, and use patterns to target specific hosts or groups of hosts in your playbooks.

The dynamic inventory feature enables you to generate inventory information dynamically from external sources, making it easier to manage large and dynamic infrastructures.

Ansible includes robust support for variables, allowing you to customize your automation for different environments, roles, and hosts.

You can define variables at different levels, such as playbooks, roles, or host inventories, and use them to parameterize your tasks and templates.

This flexibility makes it easy to reuse playbooks across multiple environments while tailoring them to specific requirements.

Ansible also supports encrypted variables, ensuring that sensitive information such as passwords and API keys can be stored securely.

In summary, Ansible is a versatile automation tool that simplifies the management and configuration of infrastructure and applications through automation.

Its agentless architecture, YAML-based playbooks, and support for variables and roles make it an accessible and powerful choice for automating a wide range of tasks and workflows.

Ansible's modular and extensible design, combined with a strong community and extensive module library, makes it an excellent tool for IT professionals and DevOps teams seeking to streamline their automation efforts and embrace infrastructure as code practices.

Ansible playbooks are at the heart of automation workflows, serving as the central building blocks for defining and orchestrating tasks, configurations, and processes.

A playbook is a structured and human-readable YAML file that outlines a series of actions to be taken on one or more target hosts.

Playbooks allow you to automate tasks, manage configurations, and execute complex workflows efficiently.

A playbook typically begins with a list of hosts or host groups, specifying where the tasks within the playbook should be applied.

Host groups can be defined in the playbook itself or referenced from an external inventory file.

Once the target hosts are defined, you can proceed to describe the tasks that should be executed on them.

Tasks are defined using Ansible modules, each representing a specific action or operation, such as installing software, configuring settings, copying files, or restarting services.

Ansible provides a vast library of built-in modules that cover a wide range of system administration and automation tasks.

To use a module within a playbook, you specify its name and provide the required parameters and values.

For example, to ensure that a specific package is installed on target hosts, you can use the "apt" module on Debian-based systems or the "yum" module on Red Hat-based systems, specifying the package name as a parameter.

Playbooks also allow you to manage variables, which provide a means of customizing playbook behavior and making it more adaptable to different environments and scenarios.

Variables can be defined at various levels, including playbook-level, role-level, and host-level.

You can use variables to parameterize your playbooks and change their behavior by supplying different variable values during playbook execution.

This flexibility allows you to reuse playbooks across different environments or hosts while tailoring configurations to specific needs.

Roles are an essential concept in Ansible playbooks, enabling you to organize and structure your automation code more effectively.

A role is a reusable collection of tasks, templates, variables, and files that can be shared and applied across multiple playbooks and projects.

Roles help modularize your automation code, promote code reuse, and simplify playbook management.

Roles can encapsulate specific functionality, such as configuring a web server, setting up a database, or managing security settings.

By using roles, you can maintain a library of well-defined automation components that can be easily integrated into your playbooks.

Roles can be created within the playbook project or downloaded from Ansible Galaxy, a repository of community-contributed roles.

Ansible Galaxy allows you to find, share, and reuse roles created by the Ansible community, saving time and effort in role development.

Tasks within playbooks can also utilize conditionals and loops to control their execution based on specific criteria or to iterate through lists of items.

Conditionals allow you to make decisions within your playbooks, executing tasks only when certain conditions are met.

For example, you can use a conditional statement to install a package on a host only if it's not already installed.

Loops, on the other hand, enable you to repeat tasks for multiple items in a list or dictionary.

This can be useful for tasks like creating multiple user accounts or configuring multiple firewall rules.

Ansible also provides handlers, which are tasks that are executed only if notified by other tasks.

Handlers are typically used to restart services or perform other actions in response to changes made during playbook execution.

For example, after modifying a configuration file, you can notify a handler to restart the associated service to apply the changes.

Playbooks support error handling mechanisms to gracefully manage exceptions and failures during execution.

You can define custom error handlers to perform specific actions when errors occur, such as sending notifications or rolling back changes.

Playbook execution can be further customized with various options and flags, allowing you to control aspects like task concurrency, verbosity, and log output.

These options make it possible to adapt playbook execution to different scenarios and requirements.

Ansible also offers a powerful feature called "roles dependencies," allowing you to define relationships between roles and control the order in which roles are applied within a playbook.

This feature is valuable when you have roles with dependencies on others, ensuring that roles are executed in the correct sequence.

Vault is another essential component of Ansible that enables the secure management of sensitive data, such as passwords, API keys, and certificates.

Vault can encrypt and store sensitive information, allowing you to reference and use these secrets securely within your playbooks and roles.

This ensures that sensitive data is protected and not exposed within your automation code.

Playbooks can be executed using the "ansible-playbook" command, specifying the playbook file to run.

Ansible will read the playbook, connect to the target hosts, and execute the defined tasks and roles.

During playbook execution, Ansible provides detailed output and logs, allowing you to monitor progress, troubleshoot issues, and verify the success of tasks.

Playbook execution is idempotent by design, meaning that running the same playbook multiple times has the same result as running it once.

This ensures that playbooks can be safely used for ongoing automation and configuration management without causing unintended changes or disruptions.

Ansible Tower, a web-based automation platform, enhances the management and orchestration of Ansible playbooks and workflows.

Ansible Tower provides features like role-based access control, job scheduling, inventory management, and a graphical dashboard for monitoring and reporting.

It offers a centralized and user-friendly interface for managing automation across large-scale environments and teams.

In summary, Ansible playbooks and automation workflows are powerful tools for automating tasks, managing configurations, and orchestrating complex processes.

Playbooks define a series of tasks, roles, variables, and dependencies that automate actions on target hosts.

Roles, conditionals, loops, handlers, and error handling provide flexibility and control within playbooks.

Vault ensures the secure management of sensitive data, and Ansible Tower enhances automation management and monitoring.

With Ansible, you can streamline and automate your IT operations, improve consistency, and embrace infrastructure as code practices to achieve greater efficiency and agility in your automation workflows.

## Chapter 7: Containerization with Docker

Containerization is a revolutionary technology that has transformed the way software is developed, deployed, and managed in modern computing environments.

At its core, containerization is a lightweight and efficient method of packaging applications and their dependencies into isolated units called containers.

Containers encapsulate an application and all its required libraries, binaries, and configuration files, ensuring consistent and predictable behavior across different environments.

The concept of containerization has gained widespread adoption due to its ability to solve various challenges in software development and operations.

Containers provide a consistent and reproducible environment for applications, eliminating the notorious "it works on my machine" problem.

By packaging an application and its dependencies together, containers ensure that what runs in development is identical to what runs in production, reducing compatibility issues and simplifying troubleshooting.

Containers are portable, allowing developers to create applications once and run them seamlessly across different platforms, from local development machines to cloud-based production environments.

This portability significantly reduces the overhead associated with managing dependencies and configurations for diverse deployment targets.

One of the key technologies enabling containerization is container runtimes, with Docker being one of the most popular and widely used container runtime engines.

Container runtimes are responsible for managing containers, including their creation, execution, and termination.

Containers share the host operating system's kernel, which makes them lightweight and efficient compared to traditional virtual machines (VMs).

While VMs emulate entire operating systems, containers leverage the host OS kernel, making them faster to start and more resource-efficient.

Containers are isolated from each other, ensuring that one container's processes and libraries do not interfere with another container's execution.

This isolation is achieved through features provided by the container runtime and the Linux kernel, such as namespaces and control groups (cgroups).

Namespaces create separate environments for processes, file systems, network interfaces, and more, while cgroups control resource allocation and usage.

Containers can be orchestrated and managed using container orchestration platforms like Kubernetes and Docker Swarm.

These platforms enable the deployment, scaling, and management of containerized applications across clusters of machines.

Orchestration platforms simplify tasks like load balancing, rolling updates, and self-healing, making it easier to manage complex microservices architectures.

Docker, a pioneer in the containerization space, introduced the Dockerfile, a simple and declarative way to define the contents and behavior of a container.

A Dockerfile contains instructions for building an image, which serves as a blueprint for creating containers.

Images are immutable, meaning that once created, they cannot be modified. To make changes, a new image must be built.

This immutability ensures consistency and repeatability in the containerization process.

Docker Hub is a popular repository for sharing and distributing Docker images, providing access to a vast library of pre-built images for various applications and services.

Containerization has revolutionized the development and deployment of applications, leading to the adoption of microservices architectures.

Microservices break down monolithic applications into smaller, independently deployable services that communicate through APIs.

Containers are an ideal technology for microservices, as each microservice can be packaged in its own container, enabling rapid development, testing, and deployment.

Containerization also facilitates continuous integration and continuous delivery (CI/CD) pipelines, allowing for automated testing and deployment of containerized applications.

This automation streamlines the software development lifecycle, from code commits to production releases.

Containers are not limited to application deployment; they are also used for development environments, enabling developers to work in consistent and isolated development containers.

Development containers provide a controlled environment with all the necessary tools and dependencies, ensuring that developers have a consistent setup across their development team.

Containerization has led to the rise of container orchestration platforms like Kubernetes, which provides powerful tools for deploying and managing containers at scale.

Kubernetes automates tasks such as load balancing, scaling, rolling updates, and self-healing, making it an essential technology for containerized applications in production.

Containerization has also accelerated the adoption of cloud-native technologies and practices.

Cloud-native applications are designed to take full advantage of cloud resources and services, and containers are a key component of this approach.

Containers can be easily orchestrated and scaled in cloud environments, enabling dynamic resource allocation and efficient utilization of cloud resources.

Containers have a significant impact on infrastructure as code (IaC) practices, as they provide a consistent unit for describing application dependencies and configurations.

IaC tools like Terraform and Ansible can be used to provision and configure infrastructure for containerized applications.

Security is a critical aspect of containerization, as containers share the host OS kernel and may pose security risks if not properly configured.

Security best practices include running containers with the least privileges necessary, regularly updating container images to patch vulnerabilities, and using container security tools to scan for known vulnerabilities.

Containerization also provides isolation at the network level, enabling containers to have their own network stack, IP address, and ports.

This network isolation allows containers to communicate with each other and external services while maintaining security and separation.

Containerization has expanded beyond the Linux ecosystem, with support for containers in Windows environments through technologies like Docker Desktop for Windows and Windows Containers.

This cross-platform support allows organizations to embrace containerization in heterogeneous environments.

In summary, containerization is a transformative technology that simplifies application development, deployment, and management by packaging applications and dependencies into isolated containers.

Containers provide consistency, portability, and efficiency, making them a fundamental building block for modern software development and operations.

Container runtimes, orchestration platforms, and cloud-native practices have propelled containerization to the forefront of technology trends, enabling organizations to embrace agility, scalability, and automation in their IT operations.

Docker has revolutionized the way containers are built, managed, and deployed in modern computing environments.

At its core, Docker is an open-source platform that simplifies the process of creating, distributing, and running containers.

Docker containers provide a consistent and portable environment for applications, making it easier to develop and deploy software across diverse infrastructure.

One of Docker's key innovations is the Dockerfile, a declarative and human-readable blueprint for creating container images.

A Dockerfile contains a series of instructions that specify the base image, copy files, install software, configure settings, and define the application to run.

Docker images are created from Dockerfiles, and they serve as the starting point for running containers.

Images are stored in a registry, such as Docker Hub or a private registry, where they can be easily shared and distributed to other users and systems.

Docker Hub, the default public registry, hosts a vast library of pre-built Docker images for various operating systems, programming languages, and software stacks.

Docker images are designed to be immutable, meaning that once built, they cannot be modified.

This immutability ensures consistency and predictability, as the same image can be used across different environments, from development to production.

Docker containers leverage the host operating system's kernel, which makes them lightweight and resource-efficient compared to traditional virtual machines (VMs).

Containers are isolated from each other using Linux kernel features like namespaces and control groups (cgroups).

Namespaces create separate environments for processes, file systems, network interfaces, and more, while cgroups control resource allocation and usage.

This isolation ensures that containers do not interfere with one another and that each container has its own runtime environment.

Docker containers can be orchestrated and managed using Docker Compose, a tool that simplifies the deployment of multi-container applications.

Docker Compose uses a YAML file to define services, networks, and volumes, allowing you to describe the components of your application stack and their dependencies.

With Docker Compose, you can start and stop multi-container applications with a single command, making it ideal for development and testing environments.

Docker containers can also be orchestrated at scale using Docker Swarm or Kubernetes, providing powerful tools for managing containerized applications in production.

Docker Swarm is Docker's native orchestration solution, while Kubernetes is a more comprehensive and widely adopted orchestration platform.

Both orchestration platforms automate tasks like load balancing, scaling, rolling updates, and service discovery, making it easier to manage complex microservices architectures.

Docker's architecture consists of a client-server model, where the Docker client communicates with the Docker daemon, which in turn interacts with the container runtime and the host operating system.

The Docker client and daemon can run on the same host or connect remotely over a network.

This client-server architecture allows Docker to be used both locally on a developer's machine and remotely on servers in data centers or the cloud.

Docker's command-line interface (CLI) provides a user-friendly way to interact with containers, images, networks, volumes, and other Docker resources.

With Docker, you can perform actions like running containers, building images, managing networks, and inspecting container logs using intuitive commands.

Docker also offers a graphical user interface (GUI) called Docker Desktop, which provides a visual interface for managing containers and images on macOS and Windows.

Docker's containerization technology has had a profound impact on software development practices.

Containers enable the packaging of applications and dependencies together, eliminating the "it works on my machine" problem that often plagues developers.

Developers can create development environments using containers that mirror production, ensuring consistent behavior from development to testing to production.

This consistency simplifies troubleshooting and minimizes issues related to differences between development and production environments.

Docker containers have become the de facto standard for microservices architectures, allowing developers to break down monolithic applications into smaller, independently deployable services.

Each microservice can be packaged in its own container, enabling rapid development, testing, and deployment of individual components.

Containerization has also accelerated the adoption of continuous integration and continuous delivery (CI/CD) practices.

CI/CD pipelines automate the building, testing, and deployment of containerized applications, reducing manual intervention and improving the speed and reliability of software releases.

Docker's container registry, Docker Hub, is a central repository for sharing and distributing Docker images.

It provides a vast library of pre-built images for various programming languages, frameworks, and services.

Developers and organizations can use Docker Hub to store, manage, and distribute their container images to teams and systems.

Docker images can be versioned, allowing you to tag and track different versions of your application or service.

This versioning ensures that you can roll back to previous versions if issues arise during deployment.

Security is a critical aspect of Docker containerization.

Docker provides security features such as user namespaces, which isolate containers from the host, and seccomp profiles, which restrict system calls to enhance security.

Container images should be regularly updated to apply security patches and address vulnerabilities.

Container security scanning tools are available to help identify known vulnerabilities in container images before they are deployed.

Docker also supports container security policies and provides features for controlling container access to system resources.

In summary, Docker has transformed containerization into a powerful technology for creating, managing, and deploying containers.

Dockerfiles and Docker images simplify the containerization process, providing consistency and immutability.

Containers are lightweight and efficient, leveraging the host OS kernel while maintaining isolation.

Orchestration platforms like Docker Swarm and Kubernetes automate container management at scale.

Docker's client-server architecture and user-friendly CLI make it accessible to both developers and operators.

Containerization has reshaped software development practices, enabling microservices architectures and CI/CD pipelines.

Docker Hub provides a central repository for sharing and distributing container images, while security features and scanning tools ensure secure containerization.

Docker has become a fundamental tool in modern software development and operations, revolutionizing the way applications are developed, packaged, and deployed.

# Chapter 8: Kubernetes for Container Orchestration

Kubernetes, often abbreviated as K8s, is a powerful open-source container orchestration platform that automates the deployment, scaling, and management of containerized applications.

Developed by Google and later donated to the Cloud Native Computing Foundation (CNCF), Kubernetes has become the de facto standard for container orchestration in cloud-native computing environments.

Kubernetes provides a flexible and extensible framework for orchestrating containers across clusters of machines, allowing organizations to build, deploy, and scale containerized applications with ease.

One of the core concepts of Kubernetes is the container, which encapsulates an application and its dependencies into a portable and isolated unit.

Containers enable developers to package their applications with all the necessary libraries, configurations, and dependencies, ensuring consistency and predictability in various environments.

Kubernetes extends the benefits of containers by automating the deployment and management of containerized applications, making it suitable for complex microservices architectures.

At the heart of Kubernetes is the control plane, which consists of several components that manage and control the cluster's operations.

The control plane components include the API server, etcd, the scheduler, the controller manager, and the cloud controller manager.

The API server is the central component that exposes the Kubernetes API, serving as the primary interface for users, administrators, and automation tools.

The etcd database stores the configuration data and state of the entire cluster, making it a critical component for ensuring the cluster's reliability and consistency.

The scheduler is responsible for placing containers onto suitable nodes within the cluster, considering factors like resource constraints, affinity, and anti-affinity rules.

The controller manager automates cluster-level functions, such as replicating applications, handling node failures, and managing various resources.

The cloud controller manager interacts with the underlying cloud provider's API to manage cloud-specific resources, like load balancers and storage volumes.

Nodes in a Kubernetes cluster are the worker machines that run containers. Each node runs an agent called the kubelet, which communicates with the control plane and ensures that containers are running as expected.

Kubernetes supports multiple container runtimes, including Docker, containerd, and CRI-O, allowing users to choose the runtime that best suits their needs.

Containers are organized into groups called pods, which are the smallest deployable units in Kubernetes.

A pod can contain one or more containers that share the same network namespace and storage volumes, making them suitable for co-locating tightly coupled application components.

To enable load balancing and external access to services within a cluster, Kubernetes introduces the concept of services.

Services define a set of pods and a policy for accessing them, ensuring that traffic is distributed evenly among the pods, even if their IP addresses or locations change.

Kubernetes also provides features for deploying and scaling applications, including replica sets, deployments, and stateful sets.

Replica sets ensure that a specified number of pod replicas are running at all times, making them useful for maintaining high availability.

Deployments manage the lifecycle of application updates, allowing for controlled rollouts and rollbacks of new versions.

Stateful sets are used for managing stateful applications that require stable network identities and persistent storage.

Kubernetes allows for dynamic scaling through the Horizontal Pod Autoscaler (HPA), which automatically adjusts the number of pod replicas based on resource utilization or custom metrics.

Ingress controllers enable the routing of external traffic to services within the cluster, providing a way to expose applications to the internet or other network resources.

Kubernetes also includes features for managing configuration and secrets, ensuring that sensitive data like API keys and passwords are stored securely and can be injected into pods as environment variables or mounted as files.

Kubernetes supports multiple storage options, including local storage, network-attached storage (NAS), and distributed storage solutions like GlusterFS and Ceph.

Kubernetes also offers persistent volumes (PVs) and persistent volume claims (PVCs) to manage storage resources and make them available to pods.

Kubernetes namespaces provide a way to logically partition a cluster, allowing teams or projects to share the same cluster while maintaining isolation.

Resource quotas and role-based access control (RBAC) enable fine-grained access control and resource allocation, ensuring that resources are used efficiently and securely.

Kubernetes extends its capabilities through a vast ecosystem of extensions, including Helm for package management, Prometheus for monitoring, and Fluentd for logging.

The flexibility and extensibility of Kubernetes make it suitable for a wide range of use cases, from small development clusters to large-scale production environments.

Kubernetes can be deployed on various cloud providers, on-premises data centers, or hybrid environments, offering flexibility and portability.

Kubernetes is actively developed and maintained by a thriving open-source community, with regular releases and updates that bring new features, enhancements, and bug fixes.

In summary, Kubernetes is a powerful container orchestration platform that simplifies the deployment, scaling, and management of containerized applications.

Kubernetes automates tasks like load balancing, scaling, and rolling updates, making it suitable for microservices architectures and cloud-native environments.

Kubernetes's control plane components, nodes, pods, services, and various resources provide a robust framework for deploying and managing containerized applications.

Kubernetes's flexibility, extensibility, and ecosystem of extensions make it a versatile choice for organizations seeking to embrace containerization and cloud-native computing.

Once you've set up a Kubernetes cluster and defined the architecture for your containerized applications, it's time to deploy those applications onto the cluster.

Kubernetes provides several methods for deploying applications, each with its own use cases and advantages.

One of the simplest ways to deploy an application is by creating a Kubernetes Deployment.

A Deployment is a high-level resource that defines the desired state of your application, including how many replicas (instances) of your application should be running at any given time.

Kubernetes then takes care of ensuring that the specified number of replicas is maintained, even in the face of node failures or other disruptions.

Deployments also support rolling updates, which allow you to change the application's image or configuration without causing downtime.

When you update a Deployment, Kubernetes gradually replaces the old replicas with new ones, ensuring a smooth transition.

Another important concept in Kubernetes is the Service.

A Service is an abstraction that provides a stable network endpoint for accessing a set of pods that belong to your application.

Services enable load balancing and automatic discovery of pods, making it possible for clients to reach your application even if the pods are spread across multiple nodes.

Services come in different types, including ClusterIP (internal to the cluster), NodePort (exposes the service on a static port on each node), and LoadBalancer (provisions an external load balancer to distribute traffic).

Choosing the right type of service depends on your application's requirements and the network architecture of your cluster.

In addition to Deployments and Services, you can also use ConfigMaps and Secrets to manage configuration and sensitive data for your applications.

ConfigMaps allow you to decouple configuration settings from your application code, making it easier to change configurations without modifying your containers.

Secrets, on the other hand, are intended for sensitive data like passwords, API keys, and certificates.

By using Secrets, you can ensure that this data is stored securely and can be safely injected into your pods.

For applications that require persistent storage, Kubernetes offers Persistent Volumes (PVs) and Persistent Volume Claims (PVCs).

PVs represent physical storage resources, while PVCs are requests for storage.

You can use PVCs to dynamically provision storage and attach it to your pods, ensuring that your application's data survives pod restarts and rescheduling.

When deploying applications, it's important to consider resource management.

Kubernetes allows you to define resource requests and limits for CPU and memory on a per-container basis.

These settings help Kubernetes schedule pods to nodes with available resources and prevent resource contention.

Kubernetes also supports Horizontal Pod Autoscaling (HPA), which automatically adjusts the number of pod replicas based on resource utilization or custom metrics.

HPA ensures that your application can handle varying loads and scale up or down as needed.

Once you've defined your application's resources and requirements, you can create a Kubernetes manifest file that describes your application's deployment, services, configurations, and other resources.

A manifest file is typically written in YAML or JSON and can be versioned alongside your application code.

To deploy your application, you can use the kubectl command-line tool, which is the primary interface for interacting with Kubernetes clusters.

kubectl allows you to apply your manifest files, check the status of your resources, and perform various other tasks related to your application.

For example, to create a Deployment and a Service from a manifest file, you can use the following command:

bashCopy code

```
kubectl apply -f your-app-manifest.yaml
```

Kubernetes will then take care of creating the necessary resources and ensuring that your application is running as specified in the manifest.

Monitoring and observability are crucial aspects of deploying applications with Kubernetes.

Kubernetes provides built-in support for collecting application and cluster-level metrics.

You can use tools like Prometheus and Grafana to gather and visualize these metrics, gaining insights into your application's performance and resource utilization.

Logs from your containers can be collected and centralized using solutions like Fluentd or the Elastic Stack (ELK).

With proper monitoring and logging in place, you can proactively identify issues, troubleshoot problems, and ensure the reliability of your applications.

Security is another critical consideration when deploying applications in Kubernetes.

Kubernetes provides a range of security features, including role-based access control (RBAC), network policies, and pod security policies. RBAC allows you to define fine-grained access controls, ensuring that only authorized users and processes can interact with your cluster's resources.

Network policies help you define rules for network traffic within your cluster, enhancing security by controlling pod-to-pod communication.

Pod security policies enable you to enforce security best practices, such as disallowing containers to run as privileged users or limiting host namespaces and capabilities.

Additionally, Kubernetes allows you to run pods with the least privileges necessary, reducing the potential attack surface.

It's essential to keep your Kubernetes clusters and applications up to date with the latest security patches and updates.

Kubernetes provides tools for rolling updates and managing application versions, making it easier to apply security fixes and improvements without causing downtime.

In summary, deploying applications with Kubernetes involves creating and managing resources like Deployments, Services, ConfigMaps, and Secrets to define your application's desired state.

Resource management, autoscaling, and manifest files are essential aspects of deploying applications effectively.

Monitoring, logging, and security considerations play a crucial role in ensuring the reliability and security of your applications in a Kubernetes environment.

By following best practices and leveraging Kubernetes's features, you can deploy and operate containerized applications with confidence, knowing that Kubernetes will manage the complexities of orchestration and scaling.

## Chapter 9: Monitoring and Scaling in the Cloud

Effective cloud monitoring and metrics collection are essential components of managing and maintaining a reliable and performant cloud infrastructure.

In today's complex and dynamic cloud environments, businesses rely on cloud services and resources to run their applications and services.

To ensure the availability, performance, and security of these applications, organizations need comprehensive monitoring solutions.

Cloud monitoring involves the continuous collection, analysis, and visualization of data from various cloud resources, including virtual machines, databases, networking components, and more.

This data, commonly referred to as metrics or telemetry, provides insights into the health and behavior of cloud resources.

Metrics can cover a wide range of aspects, such as CPU utilization, memory usage, network traffic, disk I/O, application response times, and security events.

Monitoring tools and platforms gather this data in real-time and make it available for analysis, alerting, and reporting.

Cloud providers like Amazon Web Services (AWS), Microsoft Azure, and Google Cloud offer their own native monitoring solutions.

For example, AWS provides Amazon CloudWatch, Azure offers Azure Monitor, and Google Cloud offers Google Cloud Monitoring.

These native tools allow users to collect and visualize metrics specific to the respective cloud provider's services.

Additionally, many third-party monitoring solutions are available, which provide more extensive capabilities and can work across multiple cloud providers and on-premises environments.

One of the key benefits of cloud monitoring is the ability to gain deep insights into the performance of cloud-based applications.

Monitoring tools can provide real-time visibility into application response times, latency, error rates, and the overall user experience.

This information allows organizations to identify bottlenecks, troubleshoot issues, and optimize their applications for better performance.

In addition to application performance, cloud monitoring also focuses on the health and availability of infrastructure components.

It can track the status of virtual machines, databases, load balancers, and other resources to ensure they are functioning as expected.

For example, monitoring can alert administrators when a virtual machine becomes unresponsive or when a database reaches a critical resource utilization threshold.

This proactive monitoring helps organizations minimize downtime and improve the reliability of their cloud-based services.

Security is another critical aspect of cloud monitoring.

Monitoring tools can detect and alert on security events and anomalies, such as unauthorized access attempts, unusual network traffic patterns, and potential data breaches.

These security alerts enable rapid response to threats and vulnerabilities, helping organizations protect their data and infrastructure.

Cloud monitoring also plays a significant role in cost management and optimization.

It provides insights into resource utilization and spending patterns, allowing organizations to identify areas where they can optimize their cloud spending.

For example, monitoring can help identify underutilized resources that can be terminated or downsized to reduce costs.

It can also provide recommendations for reserved instances or spot instances to save on compute costs.

In addition to real-time monitoring, cloud providers often offer long-term storage of metrics data.

This historical data is valuable for trend analysis, capacity planning, and compliance reporting.

By analyzing historical data, organizations can identify patterns, forecast future resource needs, and ensure compliance with service-level agreements (SLAs).

To effectively monitor a cloud environment, organizations should consider the following best practices:

Define Monitoring Objectives: Clearly define the objectives of your monitoring strategy, including the metrics to collect, the resources to monitor, and the desired outcomes.

Select the Right Tools: Choose monitoring tools and platforms that align with your organization's requirements, cloud provider, and application architecture.

Set Up Alerts: Configure alerting rules based on predefined thresholds or anomalies to receive notifications when issues or events occur.

Implement Dashboards: Create custom dashboards to visualize metrics and gain insights into the health and performance of your resources.

Establish Baselines: Establish baseline metrics for your applications and infrastructure to identify deviations and abnormal behavior.

Automate Remediation: Implement automated remediation actions that can respond to alerts and resolve issues without manual intervention.

Monitor Third-Party Services: Extend your monitoring to include third-party services and dependencies that your applications rely on.

Regularly Review and Update: Continuously review and update your monitoring strategy to adapt to changing cloud environments and application needs.

Cloud monitoring is not a one-size-fits-all solution; it requires customization and ongoing refinement to meet the specific needs of your organization.

Cloud providers offer a variety of monitoring services and integrations to support different use cases.

For example, AWS CloudWatch offers integrations with services like Amazon EC2, Amazon RDS, and Amazon S3, while Azure Monitor provides insights into Azure Virtual Machines, Azure SQL Database, and Azure Kubernetes Service.

Google Cloud Monitoring offers observability across Google Cloud services like Compute Engine, Google Kubernetes Engine, and Cloud Storage.

To ensure effective monitoring, organizations should align their choice of monitoring tools and integrations with their cloud provider and application stack.

In summary, cloud monitoring is a critical practice for organizations operating in cloud environments.

It provides visibility into the performance, availability, security, and cost of cloud resources and applications.

Monitoring tools and platforms collect and analyze metrics in real-time, allowing organizations to detect and respond to issues proactively.

Cloud monitoring is essential for optimizing resource utilization, ensuring security, and delivering a reliable user experience.

By following best practices and leveraging the capabilities of cloud provider-native and third-party monitoring solutions, organizations can effectively manage their cloud infrastructure and applications.

In modern cloud computing environments, the ability to dynamically adjust resources to handle varying workloads is crucial for maintaining application performance, reliability, and cost-efficiency.

Auto-scaling and load balancing are two fundamental strategies that organizations employ to meet these objectives.

Auto-scaling, as the name suggests, is the process of automatically adjusting the number of resources allocated to an application based on predefined criteria.

This can include increasing or decreasing the number of virtual machines, containers, or other compute resources as demand fluctuates.

Load balancing, on the other hand, involves distributing incoming network traffic across multiple resources, such as servers or instances, to ensure optimal utilization and prevent overloading of any single resource.

These two strategies often go hand in hand, as auto-scaling helps maintain an appropriate resource capacity, while load balancing ensures that traffic is evenly distributed to those resources.

One of the primary benefits of auto-scaling is the ability to match resource capacity to actual demand.

This prevents under-provisioning, where resources become a bottleneck during periods of high traffic, and over-provisioning, where excess resources lead to unnecessary costs during periods of low traffic.

Auto-scaling allows organizations to strike a balance, ensuring that there are enough resources to handle traffic spikes while scaling down when traffic decreases.

Auto-scaling can be implemented in various ways, depending on the cloud provider and the technology stack being used.

For instance, Amazon Web Services (AWS) offers Amazon Auto Scaling, a service that automatically adjusts the number of EC2 instances based on defined scaling policies. Similarly, Microsoft Azure provides Azure Autoscale to dynamically scale virtual machine instances.

In Kubernetes, Horizontal Pod Autoscaling (HPA) allows for the automatic adjustment of pod replicas based on CPU or custom metrics.

Auto-scaling can also be triggered by application-specific metrics, such as the number of incoming requests, response times, or queue lengths.

To achieve effective auto-scaling, organizations must carefully define scaling policies and thresholds.

These policies determine when and how resources should be scaled in or out.

For example, a common scaling policy might dictate that if the average CPU utilization of a group of virtual machines exceeds 70% for a specified duration, additional instances should be launched.

Conversely, when CPU utilization drops below 30% for a specified time, instances can be terminated to save costs.

Auto-scaling can be set up to operate reactively or proactively.

In a reactive approach, resources are scaled in response to increased demand, ensuring that the application can handle traffic peaks.

In a proactive approach, organizations may schedule auto-scaling events based on anticipated traffic patterns, such as scheduled promotions, product launches, or marketing campaigns.

Load balancing is a complementary strategy to auto-scaling, ensuring that incoming traffic is evenly distributed across available resources.

This distribution prevents individual resources from becoming overwhelmed, leading to improved application performance and fault tolerance.

Load balancers operate at the network or application layer and can distribute traffic based on various algorithms, including round-robin, least connections, and weighted distribution.

Cloud providers offer load balancing services that can be integrated with auto-scaling solutions.

For example, AWS provides Elastic Load Balancing (ELB), while Azure offers Azure Load Balancer, and Google Cloud offers Cloud Load Balancing.

These load balancers can distribute traffic across a group of virtual machines, containers, or other instances.

In addition to distributing traffic, load balancers can perform health checks on resources to ensure they are responsive and healthy.

If a resource fails a health check, the load balancer can automatically route traffic away from that resource, preventing it from impacting the overall system.

Load balancing is particularly important for applications with high availability requirements.

By spreading traffic across multiple resources, organizations can reduce the risk of downtime due to hardware failures or other issues.

Load balancers can also provide SSL termination, offloading the encryption and decryption of HTTPS traffic to improve application performance.

In cloud-native environments, container orchestration platforms like Kubernetes provide built-in load balancing capabilities.

Kubernetes services, such as ClusterIP and NodePort, automatically distribute traffic to pods within a cluster, simplifying the deployment of load-balanced applications.

Additionally, cloud-native load balancers, like AWS Application Load Balancer and Google Cloud HTTP(S) Load Balancing, are designed to work seamlessly with containerized workloads.

When implementing auto-scaling and load balancing, organizations should consider the following best practices:

Define Scaling Metrics: Clearly define the metrics that trigger auto-scaling actions, ensuring they align with the application's performance and resource utilization.

Set Conservative Thresholds: Avoid setting scaling thresholds too aggressively, as this can lead to unnecessary resource churn and increased costs.

Implement Health Checks: Configure health checks for load balancers to route traffic away from unhealthy resources, improving application reliability.

Monitor and Analyze: Continuously monitor the performance and effectiveness of auto-scaling and load balancing strategies, adjusting policies as needed.

Consider Multi-Zone Deployments: Deploy resources across multiple availability zones or regions to enhance fault tolerance and redundancy.

Leverage Auto-scaling Groups: Use auto-scaling groups or equivalent constructs to manage and scale groups of resources efficiently.

Test and Simulate: Conduct load testing and simulate traffic spikes to validate auto-scaling and load balancing configurations.

Monitor Costs: Keep an eye on the cost implications of auto-scaling, ensuring that it aligns with budget constraints.

Auto-scaling and load balancing are essential components of modern cloud infrastructure, allowing organizations to maintain application performance, reliability, and cost-efficiency.

By implementing these strategies and adhering to best practices, organizations can efficiently manage resources and ensure a seamless experience for their users.

## Chapter 10: Cloud Security and Compliance

Ensuring the security of cloud-based systems and data is paramount in today's digital landscape.

As organizations increasingly rely on cloud computing for their infrastructure and applications, adopting robust cloud security practices is essential to protect against a wide range of threats and vulnerabilities.

Cloud security encompasses a broad spectrum of measures and controls designed to safeguard cloud resources, data, and applications.

In this chapter, we'll explore a comprehensive set of best practices for cloud security to help organizations establish a strong security posture in the cloud.

One of the foundational principles of cloud security is the principle of shared responsibility.

Cloud providers, such as Amazon Web Services (AWS), Microsoft Azure, and Google Cloud, are responsible for the security of the cloud infrastructure, including the physical data centers, networks, and hardware.

However, customers are responsible for securing their data, applications, and configurations within the cloud environment.

Understanding this shared responsibility model is critical for effectively securing cloud deployments.

To start, organizations should adopt a robust identity and access management (IAM) strategy.

IAM controls access to cloud resources by defining who can access them and what actions they can perform.

Implementing the principle of least privilege (PoLP) is essential, ensuring that users and systems have only the permissions necessary to perform their tasks.

This reduces the attack surface and limits the potential damage that can occur in case of a breach.

Furthermore, organizations should enforce strong authentication mechanisms, such as multi-factor authentication (MFA), to protect against unauthorized access.

Encryption is a fundamental security measure that should be applied throughout the cloud ecosystem.

Data should be encrypted both at rest and in transit.

At rest, data should be encrypted using encryption keys managed by the cloud provider or customer-managed keys for added control.

In transit, data should be encrypted using secure protocols like HTTPS/TLS.

Organizations should also consider encrypting sensitive data within their applications and databases using encryption libraries and tools.

Encryption helps protect data from unauthorized access, whether it's stored in a database, transmitted over the network, or even stored on a mobile device.

Effective network security is another critical aspect of cloud security.

Organizations should implement network segmentation to isolate different parts of their cloud environment.

This prevents lateral movement within the network in case of a breach.

Firewalls and security groups should be configured to restrict incoming and outgoing network traffic based on specific rules.

Network monitoring and intrusion detection systems (IDS) should be in place to detect and respond to suspicious activities.

Regularly scanning for vulnerabilities in both the cloud infrastructure and application code is essential.

Cloud providers offer security scanning tools that can identify vulnerabilities in configurations and code.

Additionally, organizations should conduct regular penetration testing to assess the security of their cloud environment and applications.

By proactively identifying and addressing vulnerabilities, organizations can reduce the risk of exploitation by malicious actors.

Security monitoring and incident response capabilities should be well-established.

Cloud providers offer logging and monitoring services that capture activity and events within the cloud environment.

These logs should be regularly reviewed for signs of unauthorized access or suspicious behavior.

Automated alerting should be configured to notify security teams of potential security incidents.

An incident response plan should be in place, outlining procedures for investigating and mitigating security incidents.

Regularly testing and refining this plan is crucial for effectively responding to security breaches.

Security updates and patch management are vital to maintaining a secure cloud environment.

Organizations should regularly apply security patches and updates to the operating systems, applications, and libraries used in their cloud deployments.

Cloud providers often provide managed services to simplify patch management for their infrastructure.

However, customers are responsible for patching their virtual machines and applications.

Additionally, organizations should have a backup and disaster recovery strategy in place.

Regularly backing up data and configurations ensures that data can be recovered in case of data loss or a security incident.

Testing and validating disaster recovery plans are essential to ensure that critical services can be restored promptly.

Data retention and compliance are also key considerations in cloud security.

Organizations should establish data retention policies that align with regulatory requirements and industry standards.

Sensitive data, such as personal information or financial data, should be handled in compliance with relevant data protection regulations.

Regular audits and compliance checks help ensure that cloud deployments adhere to the necessary standards and regulations.

Lastly, employee training and awareness programs are essential components of a strong cloud security posture.

Employees should be educated about security best practices, the risks of phishing and social engineering attacks, and the importance of protecting sensitive information.

By fostering a security-aware culture, organizations can reduce the likelihood of insider threats and security lapses.

In summary, cloud security best practices encompass a range of measures and controls to protect cloud resources, data, and applications.

Understanding the shared responsibility model, implementing robust IAM, encryption, and network security measures, and regularly scanning for vulnerabilities are foundational elements of cloud security.

Security monitoring, incident response, patch management, and data retention policies contribute to a comprehensive security strategy.

Employee training and awareness programs are vital for maintaining a security-aware culture.

By following these best practices, organizations can leverage the benefits of cloud computing while minimizing security risks and ensuring the confidentiality, integrity, and availability of their data and systems.

As organizations increasingly migrate their data and applications to the cloud, the topic of regulatory compliance becomes paramount.

Regulations and compliance requirements vary across industries and regions, and organizations must navigate this complex landscape to ensure they meet their legal and industry-specific obligations.

Regulatory compliance in the cloud refers to the adherence to laws, regulations, and industry standards that govern the storage, processing, and transmission of data within cloud environments.

For many organizations, regulatory compliance is not optional but rather a legal and ethical obligation.

Non-compliance can result in severe consequences, including fines, legal actions, and damage to reputation.

Therefore, it is essential for organizations to understand the regulatory landscape, assess their compliance requirements, and implement the necessary controls in the cloud.

One of the most widely recognized regulations with global impact is the General Data Protection Regulation (GDPR).

GDPR, enacted by the European Union, applies to organizations that handle the personal data of EU residents.

It imposes strict requirements on data protection, consent, data breach notification, and the right to be forgotten.

Organizations that process personal data in the cloud, whether in data centers within or outside the EU, must ensure compliance with GDPR.

Similarly, the Health Insurance Portability and Accountability Act (HIPAA) in the United States regulates the handling of healthcare data.

Healthcare organizations that use cloud services must implement measures to protect the confidentiality and integrity of patient data.

In the financial sector, regulations such as the Payment Card Industry Data Security Standard (PCI DSS) govern the handling of credit card information.

Organizations processing credit card transactions in the cloud must adhere to PCI DSS requirements to prevent data breaches and fraud.

For organizations operating in the cloud, it is crucial to determine which regulations apply to their specific industry and geographic location.

This involves conducting a thorough compliance assessment to identify the relevant laws and standards.

Once the compliance requirements are identified, organizations must implement controls and measures to meet those requirements in the cloud.

This may involve implementing encryption, access controls, audit trails, and data retention policies, among other security measures.

Additionally, organizations should work closely with their cloud service providers to understand the shared responsibility model for compliance.

While cloud providers like Amazon Web Services (AWS), Microsoft Azure, and Google Cloud offer robust security controls and compliance certifications for their infrastructure, customers are responsible for securing their data and applications within the cloud.

Cloud providers often offer compliance documentation and audit reports, which can assist organizations in demonstrating their compliance posture to regulators and auditors.

In some cases, organizations may need to engage third-party audit and certification services to assess and verify their compliance with specific regulations.

Compliance is an ongoing process, and organizations should regularly review and update their cloud security and compliance posture as regulations evolve and their business activities change.

This includes conducting periodic risk assessments, vulnerability assessments, and penetration testing to identify and mitigate security risks in the cloud environment.

Organizations should also develop an incident response plan specific to compliance-related incidents.

In the event of a data breach or non-compliance issue, having a well-defined plan can help minimize the impact and demonstrate a commitment to resolving the issue promptly.

Furthermore, organizations should provide training and awareness programs for employees to educate them about compliance requirements and best practices.

Employees play a crucial role in data protection and compliance, and their actions can significantly impact an organization's compliance posture.

In summary, regulatory compliance in the cloud is a multifaceted and dynamic challenge.

Organizations must navigate a complex landscape of regulations and industry standards to protect sensitive data and meet legal and ethical obligations.

Understanding the regulatory landscape, assessing compliance requirements, implementing controls, and collaborating with cloud service providers are all essential elements of a successful compliance strategy.

Compliance is an ongoing process that requires vigilance, adaptability, and a commitment to maintaining a secure and compliant cloud environment.

By following best practices and staying informed about evolving regulations, organizations can leverage the benefits of cloud computing while ensuring the security and compliance of their data and systems.

## BOOK 3
## UNIX AND LINUX SYSTEM ADMINISTRATION HANDBOOK
## PERFORMANCE TUNING AND SCALING

## ROB BOTWRIGHT

# Chapter 1: Understanding System Performance Metrics

In the realm of system administration, monitoring and measuring the performance of computing systems and networks is essential for maintaining their health, optimizing their efficiency, and ensuring a seamless user experience.

Key performance metrics, often abbreviated as KPIs, provide critical insights into the behavior and state of these systems.

These metrics encompass a wide range of parameters and indicators that allow administrators to gauge the performance, availability, and capacity of their infrastructure.

Monitoring KPIs provides a basis for proactive management and problem resolution, ultimately leading to improved system performance and user satisfaction.

One of the fundamental areas of performance monitoring is system resource utilization.

This includes metrics related to CPU utilization, memory usage, disk I/O, and network bandwidth.

CPU utilization is a crucial metric that measures the percentage of CPU capacity being used by a system.

High CPU utilization can indicate a system that is under heavy load, potentially leading to performance degradation.

Monitoring memory usage is equally important, as inadequate memory can lead to slowdowns and even system crashes.

Disk I/O metrics provide insights into the read and write operations on storage devices, helping identify performance bottlenecks.

Network bandwidth usage reveals how much data is being transferred over the network, allowing administrators to detect congestion and plan for capacity expansion.

Another critical set of KPIs focuses on system responsiveness and availability.

Latency, measured in milliseconds, indicates the delay in processing requests and is vital for ensuring responsive applications.

Uptime, often expressed as a percentage, measures the amount of time a system has been available for use.

High availability is a key goal for many systems, and tracking uptime is essential to ensure service reliability.

Application-specific KPIs are also significant for assessing the performance of software applications.

Response time, which measures how quickly an application responds to user requests, directly impacts user satisfaction.

Throughput, on the other hand, measures the number of requests a system can handle within a given timeframe, reflecting its capacity.

Error rates, expressed as a percentage of failed requests or transactions, indicate the stability and quality of an application.

Monitoring these KPIs allows administrators to detect and address application performance issues promptly.

For database administrators, database-specific KPIs are indispensable for maintaining the performance and reliability of database systems.

Metrics such as query execution time, transaction throughput, and buffer cache hit ratio provide insights into database efficiency.

Administrators also monitor database storage metrics, including space utilization and I/O latency, to ensure optimal database performance.

Network administrators, on the other hand, focus on network-related KPIs to maintain the stability and performance of the network infrastructure.

These metrics include network latency, packet loss rates, and network utilization.

Latency and packet loss impact the quality of network services, while network utilization helps administrators plan for capacity upgrades.

Security-related KPIs are vital for assessing the security posture of systems and networks.

These metrics encompass indicators such as the number of security incidents, successful and failed login attempts, and the volume of incoming and outgoing network traffic.

Monitoring security KPIs allows administrators to detect and respond to security threats promptly.

Capacity planning KPIs provide a forward-looking perspective on infrastructure requirements.

These metrics include trends in resource utilization, forecasted growth rates, and estimated time until resource exhaustion.

Capacity planning helps administrators anticipate resource shortages and plan for upgrades or optimizations.

Administrators also monitor environmental KPIs related to the physical infrastructure, such as temperature, humidity, and power usage.

Out-of-spec environmental conditions can lead to hardware failures and system downtime.

Application performance KPIs, including user satisfaction ratings and user engagement metrics, offer insights into the end-user experience.

User satisfaction ratings, often collected through surveys or feedback forms, provide qualitative feedback on the quality of service.

User engagement metrics, such as page views, click-through rates, and session duration, help assess the usability and effectiveness of web applications.

These KPIs enable administrators to align system performance with user expectations.

It is essential for organizations to define their own set of KPIs based on their specific objectives, priorities, and the nature of their systems and applications.

Once KPIs are established, monitoring tools and solutions are employed to collect and visualize data.

These tools can range from open-source solutions like Nagios and Zabbix to commercial products like SolarWinds and Datadog.

Cloud providers also offer monitoring services that can capture and analyze KPIs for cloud-based resources.

Monitoring tools provide dashboards and alerts that enable administrators to stay informed about the state of their systems in real-time.

KPI data is collected from various sources, including system logs, performance counters, and sensors.

This data is then processed and presented in a format that allows administrators to identify trends, anomalies, and areas requiring attention.

Alerting mechanisms are often configured to notify administrators when KPIs exceed predefined thresholds or when abnormal patterns are detected.

The proactive nature of performance monitoring allows administrators to take preventive measures and address issues before they impact users.

In summary, key performance metrics (KPIs) are essential for system administrators to monitor and manage the performance, availability, and capacity of computing systems and networks.

These metrics encompass a wide range of parameters, including resource utilization, system responsiveness, application performance, security, and capacity planning.

Establishing and monitoring KPIs provide administrators with valuable insights and enable them to make informed decisions to optimize system performance and user satisfaction.

Choosing the right monitoring tools and solutions, configuring alerts, and proactively addressing issues are integral parts of effective KPI-based performance management.

In the realm of system administration, monitoring and measuring the performance of computing systems and networks is essential for maintaining their health, optimizing their efficiency, and ensuring a seamless user experience.

Key performance metrics, often abbreviated as KPIs, provide critical insights into the behavior and state of these systems.

These metrics encompass a wide range of parameters and indicators that allow administrators to gauge the performance, availability, and capacity of their infrastructure.

Monitoring KPIs provides a basis for proactive management and problem resolution, ultimately leading to improved system performance and user satisfaction.

One of the fundamental areas of performance monitoring is system resource utilization.

This includes metrics related to CPU utilization, memory usage, disk I/O, and network bandwidth.

CPU utilization is a crucial metric that measures the percentage of CPU capacity being used by a system.

High CPU utilization can indicate a system that is under heavy load, potentially leading to performance degradation.

Monitoring memory usage is equally important, as inadequate memory can lead to slowdowns and even system crashes.

Disk I/O metrics provide insights into the read and write operations on storage devices, helping identify performance bottlenecks.

Network bandwidth usage reveals how much data is being transferred over the network, allowing administrators to detect congestion and plan for capacity expansion.

Another critical set of KPIs focuses on system responsiveness and availability.

Latency, measured in milliseconds, indicates the delay in processing requests and is vital for ensuring responsive applications.

Uptime, often expressed as a percentage, measures the amount of time a system has been available for use.

High availability is a key goal for many systems, and tracking uptime is essential to ensure service reliability.

Application-specific KPIs are also significant for assessing the performance of software applications.

Response time, which measures how quickly an application responds to user requests, directly impacts user satisfaction.

Throughput, on the other hand, measures the number of requests a system can handle within a given timeframe, reflecting its capacity.

Error rates, expressed as a percentage of failed requests or transactions, indicate the stability and quality of an application.

Monitoring these KPIs allows administrators to detect and address application performance issues promptly.

For database administrators, database-specific KPIs are indispensable for maintaining the performance and reliability of database systems.

Metrics such as query execution time, transaction throughput, and buffer cache hit ratio provide insights into database efficiency.

Administrators also monitor database storage metrics, including space utilization and I/O latency, to ensure optimal database performance.

Network administrators, on the other hand, focus on network-related KPIs to maintain the stability and performance of the network infrastructure.

These metrics include network latency, packet loss rates, and network utilization.

Latency and packet loss impact the quality of network services, while network utilization helps administrators plan for capacity upgrades.

Security-related KPIs are vital for assessing the security posture of systems and networks.

These metrics encompass indicators such as the number of security incidents, successful and failed login attempts, and the volume of incoming and outgoing network traffic.

Monitoring security KPIs allows administrators to detect and respond to security threats promptly.

Capacity planning KPIs provide a forward-looking perspective on infrastructure requirements.

These metrics include trends in resource utilization, forecasted growth rates, and estimated time until resource exhaustion.

Capacity planning helps administrators anticipate resource shortages and plan for upgrades or optimizations.

Administrators also monitor environmental KPIs related to the physical infrastructure, such as temperature, humidity, and power usage.

Out-of-spec environmental conditions can lead to hardware failures and system downtime.

Application performance KPIs, including user satisfaction ratings and user engagement metrics, offer insights into the end-user experience.

User satisfaction ratings, often collected through surveys or feedback forms, provide qualitative feedback on the quality of service.

User engagement metrics, such as page views, click-through rates, and session duration, help assess the usability and effectiveness of web applications.

These KPIs enable administrators to align system performance with user expectations.

It is essential for organizations to define their own set of KPIs based on their specific objectives, priorities, and the nature of their systems and applications.

Once KPIs are established, monitoring tools and solutions are employed to collect and visualize data.

These tools can range from open-source solutions like Nagios and Zabbix to commercial products like SolarWinds and Datadog.

Cloud providers also offer monitoring services that can capture and analyze KPIs for cloud-based resources.

Monitoring tools provide dashboards and alerts that enable administrators to stay informed about the state of their systems in real-time.

KPI data is collected from various sources, including system logs, performance counters, and sensors.

This data is then processed and presented in a format that allows administrators to identify trends, anomalies, and areas requiring attention.

Alerting mechanisms are often configured to notify administrators when KPIs exceed predefined thresholds or when abnormal patterns are detected.

The proactive nature of performance monitoring allows administrators to take preventive measures and address issues before they impact users.

In summary, key performance metrics (KPIs) are essential for system administrators to monitor and manage the performance, availability, and capacity of computing systems and networks.

These metrics encompass a wide range of parameters, including resource utilization, system responsiveness, application performance, security, and capacity planning.

Establishing and monitoring KPIs provide administrators with valuable insights and enable them to make informed decisions to optimize system performance and user satisfaction.

Choosing the right monitoring tools and solutions, configuring alerts, and proactively addressing issues are integral parts of effective KPI-based performance management.

In the world of system administration, the ability to monitor and analyze the performance and health of computing systems and networks is a critical aspect of ensuring their reliability and efficiency.

Monitoring and analysis tools play a pivotal role in providing administrators with the insights and data they need to make informed decisions, troubleshoot issues, and optimize their infrastructure.

These tools encompass a wide range of capabilities, from real-time performance monitoring to historical data analysis, and they are essential components of a system administrator's toolkit.

Real-time monitoring tools provide administrators with immediate visibility into the current state of their systems and networks.

These tools continuously collect data on various performance metrics, such as CPU utilization, memory usage, network bandwidth, and disk I/O.

Real-time dashboards and graphs allow administrators to visualize this data, making it easy to identify anomalies, spikes, or trends that may require attention.

For example, a sudden spike in CPU utilization may indicate a resource-intensive task or application, while a drop in network bandwidth could signal a network congestion issue.

Alerting mechanisms within these tools can be configured to notify administrators when predefined thresholds are exceeded, enabling them to respond promptly to emerging issues.

Historical data analysis tools, on the other hand, provide a deeper understanding of system performance over time.

These tools store and retain historical performance data, allowing administrators to track trends, identify patterns, and conduct root cause analysis for past incidents.

By examining historical data, administrators can gain insights into long-term performance degradation, capacity planning needs, and the impact of changes or upgrades.

Historical analysis can help answer questions such as, "Has CPU utilization been steadily increasing over the past month?" or "What caused the performance degradation that occurred last week?"

Capacity planning tools are a subset of historical analysis tools that focus on predicting future resource needs.

These tools use historical data to forecast resource utilization and help administrators make informed decisions about capacity upgrades or optimizations.

Capacity planning is crucial for ensuring that computing resources, such as CPU, memory, and storage, are adequately provisioned to meet current and future demands.

Network monitoring tools specialize in tracking the performance and availability of network infrastructure.

They capture data related to network latency, packet loss rates, bandwidth utilization, and device status.

Network administrators rely on these tools to detect network issues, identify bottlenecks, and troubleshoot connectivity problems.

Effective network monitoring is essential for ensuring a reliable and responsive network, particularly in organizations where network downtime can have severe consequences.

Security monitoring tools are designed to detect and respond to security threats and incidents.

These tools analyze security-related data, such as logs, events, and alerts, to identify suspicious or malicious activities.

Security monitoring tools often include intrusion detection systems (IDS), intrusion prevention systems (IPS), and security information and event management (SIEM) solutions.

They provide administrators with the means to detect unauthorized access, data breaches, and other security breaches promptly.

Application performance monitoring (APM) tools focus on the performance of software applications and services.

They capture data on response times, throughput, error rates, and user satisfaction.

APM tools are invaluable for identifying application performance bottlenecks, optimizing code, and ensuring a seamless user experience.

Database monitoring tools cater specifically to the performance and health of database systems.

They collect data on query execution times, transaction rates, cache hit ratios, and storage usage.

Database administrators rely on these tools to identify slow queries, optimize database performance, and ensure data integrity.

Cloud monitoring tools are designed for organizations that leverage cloud computing services.

These tools provide visibility into the performance and availability of cloud-based resources and services.

Cloud monitoring tools capture data related to virtual machines, storage, databases, and cloud-based applications.

They help organizations monitor and optimize their cloud infrastructure while ensuring cost-effective resource utilization.

Environmental monitoring tools focus on the physical aspects of the data center or server room.

They measure factors such as temperature, humidity, power consumption, and airflow.

Environmental monitoring is essential for preventing hardware failures due to adverse conditions and for maintaining a stable computing environment.

Log analysis tools are used to collect, aggregate, and analyze log data generated by various systems, applications, and devices.

These tools help administrators detect issues, troubleshoot problems, and gain insights into system behavior.

Log analysis is particularly valuable for security and compliance purposes, as it can uncover suspicious or anomalous activities.

Open-source and commercial monitoring and analysis tools are available to suit various needs and budgets.

Prominent open-source options include Nagios, Zabbix, Cacti, and the Elastic Stack (Elasticsearch, Logstash, Kibana).

Commercial solutions, such as SolarWinds, Datadog, New Relic, and Splunk, offer additional features and support.

Many cloud providers also offer monitoring and analysis services for their cloud-based resources, making it easy for organizations to monitor their cloud deployments.

The choice of monitoring and analysis tools depends on factors such as the organization's size, budget, specific monitoring requirements, and the complexity of its infrastructure.

Integrating monitoring and analysis tools into the system administration workflow is a strategic decision that can lead to improved system performance, greater reliability, and reduced downtime.

Implementing these tools allows administrators to proactively manage their systems, detect and resolve issues efficiently, and make data-driven decisions to optimize their infrastructure.

Furthermore, these tools are essential for ensuring compliance, enhancing security, and delivering a seamless user experience.

In summary, monitoring and analysis tools are indispensable assets for system administrators.

They provide real-time insights into system performance, historical data analysis for troubleshooting and capacity planning, and specialized capabilities for network, security, application, database, cloud, environmental, and log monitoring.

Choosing the right tools and integrating them into the system administration workflow is essential for maintaining the health and efficiency of computing systems and networks.

**Chapter 2: Profiling and Benchmarking Tools**

In the realm of system administration and software development, optimizing the performance of applications and systems is a continuous pursuit.

Profiling, as a technique, plays a crucial role in analyzing and improving the efficiency of software and hardware components.

Profiling is the process of measuring and analyzing the execution of a program or system to identify performance bottlenecks, resource utilization, and areas for improvement.

It provides valuable insights into the behavior of an application, enabling administrators and developers to make informed decisions to enhance performance.

Profiling can be applied at various levels, including application-level profiling, system-level profiling, and hardware-level profiling.

At the application level, profiling tools gather data about the execution of a specific software application.

These tools measure aspects such as function execution times, memory usage, and CPU utilization.

Application-level profiling helps identify slow or resource-intensive code segments, allowing developers to optimize their software for better performance.

System-level profiling extends the analysis to the entire operating system and all running processes.

This form of profiling provides a holistic view of system behavior, including resource allocation, context switches, and I/O operations.

System-level profiling is essential for identifying system-wide performance issues and bottlenecks that may impact multiple applications.

Hardware-level profiling focuses on the hardware components of a system, such as the CPU, memory, and storage.

Profiling tools at this level provide data on hardware utilization, cache hits and misses, and memory access patterns.

Hardware-level profiling is valuable for understanding how software interacts with the underlying hardware and can lead to optimizations at both the software and hardware levels.

One of the primary goals of profiling is to identify performance bottlenecks.

A bottleneck is a point in the system where the flow of data or execution is significantly slowed down, limiting overall system performance.

Profiling tools can pinpoint bottlenecks by analyzing which functions or processes consume the most resources or take the most time to execute.

Once bottlenecks are identified, administrators and developers can focus their efforts on optimizing these critical areas to improve system performance.

Another key aspect of profiling is resource utilization analysis.

Profiling tools can measure how various system resources are utilized during program execution.

This includes monitoring CPU usage, memory allocation and deallocation, I/O operations, and network activity.

Resource utilization analysis helps identify inefficiencies, such as memory leaks or excessive CPU usage, allowing for resource optimization.

Memory profiling, in particular, is a valuable technique for identifying memory-related issues in software.

Memory leaks, where allocated memory is not properly released, can lead to gradual performance degradation and even application crashes.

Memory profiling tools track memory allocations and deallocations, helping developers identify and fix memory leaks.

Additionally, profiling tools can analyze the behavior of multi-threaded applications.

Multi-threaded programming introduces complexities related to thread synchronization, resource contention, and race conditions.

Profiling can reveal performance bottlenecks and synchronization issues in multi-threaded code, enabling developers to write more efficient and thread-safe software.

Beyond performance analysis, profiling can also assist in the detection of software bugs and security vulnerabilities.

Profiling tools may uncover unexpected behavior, such as buffer overflows, null pointer dereferences, or infinite loops, which can lead to application crashes or security breaches.

By identifying these issues early in the development process, developers can write more robust and secure code.

Profiling is not limited to software applications; it can also be applied to system administration tasks.

For example, administrators can use profiling to analyze the performance of network services, file system operations, and resource usage on servers.

Profiling server components can help identify configuration issues, resource contention, and potential security vulnerabilities.

Profiling tools vary in complexity and capabilities, ranging from simple command-line utilities to comprehensive integrated development environment (IDE) tools.

Common profiling tools for various programming languages include:

C/C++: gprof, Valgrind, perf

Java: VisualVM, YourKit Java Profiler, JProfiler

Python: cProfile, Pyflame, line_profiler

.NET: Visual Studio Profiler, JetBrains dotTrace

These tools provide a wide range of features, including real-time monitoring, data visualization, and support for various profiling techniques.

Choosing the right profiling tool depends on factors such as the programming language, the complexity of the application, and the specific performance aspects to be analyzed.

It is important to note that profiling introduces some overhead, as it collects data during program execution.

Therefore, profiling should be used selectively, focusing on areas of interest or suspected performance issues, to minimize the impact on the application's performance.

Profiling is an iterative process, where administrators and developers continuously analyze, optimize, and retest their software and systems.

By using profiling as a diagnostic and improvement tool, organizations can achieve better application performance, reduced resource consumption, and improved user experiences.

In summary, profiling is a valuable technique for analyzing and optimizing the performance of software applications and systems.

It provides insights into performance bottlenecks, resource utilization, and areas for improvement at the application, system, and hardware levels.

Profiling tools are essential for identifying performance issues, memory leaks, multi-threading problems, and security vulnerabilities in software.

By using profiling as part of their development and system administration workflows, organizations can deliver more efficient, reliable, and secure software and services.

Benchmarking is a systematic process used to compare the performance of a system, application, or component against established standards or other systems to identify areas for improvement.

This technique plays a vital role in evaluating and optimizing the efficiency, reliability, and quality of various aspects of computing environments.

Benchmarking provides organizations with a structured approach to measure, analyze, and enhance performance across different domains.

Benchmarking can be applied to a wide range of computing environments, from hardware and software systems to network infrastructure and cloud services.

One of the primary objectives of benchmarking is to establish performance baselines.

Baseline measurements serve as reference points against which future performance can be compared, allowing organizations to track improvements or identify regressions over time.

Performance benchmarks are typically created by executing a series of standardized tests or workloads under controlled conditions.

These tests are designed to simulate real-world usage scenarios and generate data that quantifies system performance.

Hardware benchmarking focuses on evaluating the capabilities of computer hardware components, such as CPUs, GPUs, memory modules, and storage devices.

Benchmarking tools measure parameters like processing speed, memory bandwidth, disk read/write speeds, and graphics rendering capabilities.

Hardware vendors often use benchmark results to showcase the performance of their products and help customers make informed purchasing decisions.

Software benchmarking, on the other hand, assesses the performance of software applications, libraries, or frameworks.

These benchmarks measure factors like application startup time, response time, throughput, and resource utilization.

Software developers use benchmarking to identify performance bottlenecks, optimize code, and ensure that their applications meet performance expectations.

Network benchmarking evaluates the performance and reliability of network infrastructure, including routers, switches, and network protocols.

Network benchmarking tests may include assessing latency, packet loss, bandwidth, and the ability to handle a high volume of network traffic.

Network administrators use benchmarking to ensure that network components meet service level agreements (SLAs) and can handle expected loads without degradation.

Cloud benchmarking assesses the performance and cost-effectiveness of cloud services and providers.

Cloud benchmarks measure parameters like virtual machine provisioning time, data transfer speeds, and cost per unit of computation.

Organizations use cloud benchmarking to choose the right cloud provider, optimize resource allocation, and control cloud-related expenses.

Benchmarking can also be categorized based on the focus of the evaluation.

Some benchmarks emphasize synthetic or artificial workloads that are designed to stress specific system components.

Synthetic benchmarks generate unrealistic loads to test hardware or software limitations.

For example, a synthetic CPU benchmark might calculate prime numbers continuously to evaluate a CPU's processing power under maximum load.

Other benchmarks prioritize real-world workloads that mimic actual usage scenarios.

Real-world benchmarks provide more accurate insights into how a system or application will perform in practical situations.

For instance, a database benchmark might measure the time it takes to process a series of typical database queries.

Benchmarking can be further classified into microbenchmarking and macrobenchmarking.

Microbenchmarking involves testing small, isolated code segments or functions to assess their performance.

Microbenchmarks are fine-grained and focus on specific operations, such as sorting algorithms or encryption routines.

Macrobenchmarking, on the other hand, evaluates the performance of complete applications or systems.

Macrobenchmarks provide a broader view of overall system performance and are often used to assess the end-to-end performance of a system.

Benchmarking tools and frameworks play a crucial role in the benchmarking process.

These tools automate the execution of benchmarks, collect performance data, and generate reports.

Common benchmarking tools include:

SPEC (Standard Performance Evaluation Corporation) benchmarks for measuring the performance of CPUs, compilers, and web servers.

Apache JMeter for load testing and performance testing of web applications.

Geekbench for cross-platform benchmarking of CPUs, GPUs, and memory.

iozone for file system benchmarking.

TPC (Transaction Processing Performance Council) benchmarks for assessing database performance.

Phoronix Test Suite for comprehensive Linux benchmarking.

The choice of benchmarking tools depends on the specific requirements of the benchmark, the target platform, and the desired level of detail in performance analysis.

Benchmarking results are typically presented in the form of performance metrics or scores.

These scores can be used to compare the performance of different systems or components objectively.

For example, a higher benchmark score may indicate better performance in a specific area.

However, it is essential to interpret benchmark results in the context of the specific workload or use case relevant to the organization.

Benchmarking results can be influenced by various factors, including system configuration, hardware and software versions, and benchmarking methodology.

Therefore, organizations should ensure that benchmarking tests are conducted under consistent conditions and that results are reproducible.

Benchmarking is not a one-time activity but an ongoing process.

As technology evolves, organizations need to revisit their benchmarks periodically to adapt to changing hardware, software, and workload requirements.

Benchmarking is not without challenges and limitations.

Choosing the right benchmarks that accurately represent the organization's real-world use cases can be challenging.

Additionally, benchmarking tools and workloads may not cover every aspect of a system's performance.

Overreliance on benchmarks can lead to tunnel vision, as organizations may prioritize performance metrics at the expense of other critical factors like security, reliability, and scalability.

Benchmarking also requires careful consideration of ethical and legal aspects, as publishing benchmark results can lead to competitive concerns and intellectual property issues.

In summary, benchmarking is a valuable technique for measuring and improving the performance of computing systems, applications, and networks.

It provides organizations with the means to establish performance baselines, identify performance bottlenecks, and make informed decisions to optimize their computing environments.

Benchmarking spans various domains, including hardware, software, network infrastructure, and cloud services, and can be tailored to focus on synthetic or real-world workloads.

Benchmarking tools and methodologies play a crucial role in automating benchmark execution and analyzing performance data.

Organizations should use benchmarking as part of their continuous improvement efforts while considering the limitations and ethical considerations associated with this practice.

Benchmarking serves as a valuable tool in the pursuit of better performance, efficiency, and quality in the ever-evolving landscape of computing.

## Chapter 3: Kernel Tuning and Optimization

The kernel of an operating system serves as the core component that manages system resources, facilitates communication between hardware and software, and ensures the overall stability and performance of a computer system.

One of the critical aspects of kernel management is the configuration of kernel parameters, which are tunable settings that govern the behavior of the kernel and its interaction with hardware and software components.

Kernel parameters allow system administrators to customize and optimize the kernel's operation to meet specific system requirements and performance goals.

These parameters cover a wide range of functionalities, from memory management and process scheduling to I/O operations and network protocols.

Kernel parameters can be divided into two primary categories: compile-time parameters and runtime parameters.

Compile-time parameters are configured when the kernel is built from source code, and they determine the kernel's fundamental characteristics and features.

System administrators typically customize compile-time parameters by modifying the kernel source code or configuration files before compiling the kernel.

These parameters are set during the kernel's initial installation or update and remain fixed until the kernel is recompiled.

Examples of compile-time parameters include the selection of device drivers, filesystem support, and architectural features.

Runtime parameters, on the other hand, are adjusted while the system is running, allowing system administrators to fine-tune the kernel's behavior without the need to rebuild or reboot the entire system.

Runtime parameters are stored in kernel data structures and can be modified using system utilities such as sysctl on Unix-like systems or the Windows Registry on Windows systems.

Runtime parameters are temporary and apply only for the current system session; they revert to their default values upon system reboot.

A core aspect of kernel parameter configuration is understanding the available parameters and their impact on system behavior.

System administrators must be familiar with the documentation and resources specific to their operating system to make informed decisions when configuring kernel parameters.

Common categories of kernel parameters include:

Memory Management: Parameters related to memory allocation, swapping, and management, including settings for the allocation of physical and virtual memory, swap space usage, and memory thresholds.

Process Scheduling: Parameters that govern the scheduling of processes, threads, and tasks within the system, influencing factors like CPU time-sharing, process priority, and context switching behavior.

I/O and Filesystems: Parameters related to input and output operations and filesystem behavior, such as disk I/O buffer sizes, file cache settings, and filesystem-specific options.

Network and Networking Protocols: Parameters that control network-related operations, including network stack behavior, socket settings, and network protocol configurations.

Security and Permissions: Parameters that affect system security and access control, including permissions, access control lists (ACLs), and security modules.

Performance Tuning: Parameters for optimizing system performance, including tuning for specific workloads, adjusting kernel timer frequencies, and setting interrupt handling priorities.

Configuring kernel parameters requires careful consideration, as improper settings can lead to system instability, performance degradation, or security vulnerabilities.

Administrators must strike a balance between optimizing for performance and ensuring system stability and security.

It is crucial to document any changes made to kernel parameters, as this documentation can aid in troubleshooting issues, auditing system configurations, and reproducing specific system states.

When configuring kernel parameters, it is recommended to follow best practices and guidelines provided by the operating system's documentation and the recommendations of hardware and software vendors.

Additionally, system administrators should conduct thorough testing and validation of parameter changes in non-production environments to assess their impact on system behavior and performance.

Kernel parameters often interact with one another, so understanding the dependencies and consequences of parameter changes is essential.

System administrators should also be aware of potential conflicts between kernel parameters and user-level application settings, as these can affect the overall system behavior.

In some cases, user-level applications may override or conflict with kernel parameters, requiring coordination and troubleshooting to resolve.

Operating systems may provide tools and utilities to view and modify kernel parameters conveniently.

For example, in Unix-like systems, the sysctl command allows users to query and modify runtime kernel parameters.

In Windows, the Windows Registry Editor provides access to kernel and system settings.

Additionally, configuration management tools and scripts can be employed to automate the management of kernel parameters across multiple systems in a consistent and controlled manner.

In summary, kernel parameters and their configuration play a crucial role in system administration, allowing administrators to customize and optimize the behavior of the kernel to meet specific system requirements and performance goals.

Understanding the available kernel parameters, their impact on system behavior, and best practices for configuration is essential for effective system management.

Careful consideration, documentation, and testing of parameter changes are vital to ensuring system stability, performance, and security.

System administrators should stay informed about updates, patches, and security advisories related to kernel parameters to maintain a secure and well-tuned computing environment.

Configuring kernel parameters is both a science and an art, requiring a balance between performance optimization and the preservation of system reliability and security.

# Chapter 4: File System Performance Tuning

Efficiency is a fundamental consideration in system administration, as it directly impacts the utilization of hardware resources, energy consumption, and overall system performance.

Efficient system management strives to achieve optimal resource allocation, minimize wastage, and ensure that the system operates at peak performance while conserving energy and reducing operational costs.

Tuning for system efficiency involves a holistic approach that encompasses various aspects of the computing environment.

At the heart of system efficiency lies the judicious allocation of system resources, including CPU, memory, storage, and network bandwidth.

Efficient resource allocation ensures that each component operates near its capacity, avoiding underutilization or overutilization, which can lead to performance bottlenecks or wasted resources.

The first step in resource allocation tuning is understanding the workload and usage patterns of the system.

By analyzing historical data and monitoring system performance, administrators can gain insights into resource demands and identify areas where resource allocation can be adjusted.

For example, if a web server experiences spikes in traffic during specific hours, administrators can allocate additional CPU and memory resources during those times to maintain responsiveness.

Virtualization and cloud technologies have further enhanced resource allocation flexibility, enabling administrators to dynamically allocate and deallocate resources based on workload demands.

Efficiency in resource allocation also involves optimizing the allocation of virtual resources, ensuring that virtual machines (VMs) receive the appropriate amount of CPU, memory, and storage to meet their requirements.

Efficient memory management is a critical component of system efficiency.

Memory is a finite and often shared resource, and its proper allocation and utilization are essential for system performance.

Administrators can tune memory allocation by adjusting parameters like swap space size, page cache settings, and memory allocation policies.

Efficient memory usage minimizes unnecessary swapping of data between RAM and disk, reducing latency and improving overall system responsiveness.

Storage efficiency is another crucial consideration in system tuning.

Storage resources can quickly become a bottleneck if not managed efficiently.

Administrators can optimize storage by implementing techniques such as data deduplication, compression, and thin provisioning to reduce storage consumption.

Efficient storage management also involves the strategic placement of data on various types of storage devices, such as high-performance SSDs for frequently accessed data and slower, cost-effective HDDs for archival storage.

Network efficiency is paramount in modern computing environments, where network traffic can be a significant source of resource contention.

Efficient network tuning involves optimizing network protocols, bandwidth allocation, and traffic prioritization.

Administrators can adjust network parameters to reduce latency, maximize throughput, and ensure that critical applications receive the necessary bandwidth.

Techniques like Quality of Service (QoS) can be employed to prioritize network traffic based on application requirements.

Energy efficiency is an increasingly critical aspect of system tuning, as organizations seek to reduce their carbon footprint and energy costs.

Efficient power management strategies include optimizing CPU power states, implementing dynamic voltage and frequency scaling (DVFS), and using hardware features like wake-on-LAN and power-saving modes.

Efficiency in power management not only reduces energy consumption but also prolongs hardware lifespan and reduces heat generation, which can improve overall system reliability.

Virtualization technologies like server consolidation and workload migration contribute to energy efficiency by allowing administrators to consolidate workloads onto fewer physical servers, reducing energy consumption and cooling requirements.

Efficient system efficiency tuning also extends to software optimization.

Application performance can have a significant impact on overall system efficiency.

Administrators should regularly assess and optimize software applications by identifying and addressing performance bottlenecks, optimizing code, and ensuring that applications are efficiently using system resources.

Efficient software deployment practices, such as containerization and microservices architectures, promote resource-efficient application execution by isolating applications and their dependencies, reducing resource contention, and enabling rapid scaling.

Monitoring and performance analysis tools are essential for system administrators to identify areas where efficiency improvements can be made.

These tools provide insights into resource utilization, application performance, and system health, enabling administrators to make informed tuning decisions.

Efficient monitoring and analysis help detect abnormal behavior, performance anomalies, and potential bottlenecks before they impact system efficiency.

Regularly reviewing and interpreting monitoring data is a proactive approach to maintaining and improving system efficiency.

It allows administrators to anticipate resource demands, plan capacity upgrades, and implement performance enhancements in a timely manner.

In summary, tuning for system efficiency is a multifaceted endeavor that encompasses resource allocation, memory management, storage optimization, network efficiency, energy conservation, and software performance.

Efficient system management is essential for ensuring that hardware resources are utilized optimally, operational costs are minimized, and the system operates reliably and responsively.

Administrators must adopt a holistic approach to system efficiency tuning, considering the interplay between hardware, software, and workload characteristics.

Efficiency tuning requires ongoing monitoring, analysis, and adjustment to adapt to changing requirements and technological advancements.

By prioritizing system efficiency, organizations can achieve better resource utilization, reduced operational costs, improved sustainability, and enhanced user experiences.

## Chapter 5: Memory Management and Optimization

File systems are a critical component of modern computing environments, serving as the foundation for storing, organizing, and accessing data.
The choice of file system type can significantly impact system performance and efficiency.
Understanding the characteristics and performance attributes of different file system types is essential for system administrators and architects.
File systems are responsible for managing data storage, including files, directories, and metadata.
They provide an organized structure for storing and retrieving data, enabling efficient data access and management.
File system performance is influenced by several factors, including the file system type, storage media, file system configuration, and workload characteristics.
There are various file system types available, each designed to meet specific use cases and requirements.
Common file system types include:
Ext4: A widely used file system in Linux distributions, known for its reliability and backward compatibility with its predecessor, Ext3.
NTFS: The default file system for Windows operating systems, offering features like access control lists (ACLs) and file compression.
FAT32: A legacy file system suitable for removable storage devices and cross-platform compatibility, but with limitations on file size and partition size.
APFS: Apple's file system for macOS and iOS, known for its encryption and snapshot capabilities.

ZFS: A powerful and feature-rich file system used in various Unix-like operating systems, offering features like data deduplication, compression, and advanced storage management.

XFS: A high-performance file system designed for large-scale storage and high-throughput workloads, often used in Linux environments.

Btrfs: A modern file system with support for features like snapshots, checksums, and RAID-like capabilities, designed for Linux distributions.

ReFS: Resilient File System, introduced in Windows Server, optimized for data integrity and fault tolerance.

Each file system type has its strengths and weaknesses, making it essential to choose the right file system for a particular use case.

File system performance is influenced by the underlying storage media.

Traditional spinning hard disk drives (HDDs) offer different performance characteristics compared to solid-state drives (SSDs).

SSDs provide faster data access times, lower latency, and improved overall system responsiveness compared to HDDs, making them suitable for applications that demand high I/O performance.

File system configuration and tuning also play a significant role in achieving optimal performance.

Administrators can adjust file system parameters and mount options to optimize performance for specific workloads.

For example, adjusting the block size or enabling write-back caching can enhance file system performance for certain applications.

The workload characteristics of a system heavily influence file system performance.

Different workloads, such as database access, web serving, file sharing, or scientific computing, place varying demands on the file system.

Some workloads involve frequent small reads and writes, while others require large sequential data access.

File system tuning should align with the specific demands of the workload to achieve optimal performance.

Caching mechanisms, such as read-ahead and write-behind caching, can significantly improve file system performance by reducing disk I/O operations.

These mechanisms cache frequently accessed data in memory, reducing the need to read or write to disk, which is a slow and resource-intensive operation.

File system journaling is another critical aspect of performance and data integrity.

Journaling helps recover file system consistency after unexpected system crashes or power failures but may introduce some performance overhead.

Administrators can adjust journaling settings to balance data integrity and performance.

Advanced file system features, such as data deduplication, compression, and encryption, can impact performance.

For example, data deduplication reduces storage space usage by eliminating duplicate data, but the deduplication process consumes CPU and memory resources.

Compression can reduce storage costs but may increase CPU usage during read and write operations.

Encryption, while essential for data security, can introduce additional computational overhead.

Choosing the appropriate file system features and settings depends on the specific requirements of the system and workload.

Efficient data management strategies, such as file organization and data tiering, also contribute to file system performance. Organizing data into logical directories and hierarchies can simplify data access and improve data retrieval times.

Data tiering involves moving less frequently accessed data to slower, more cost-effective storage tiers, such as archival storage or cloud storage, while keeping frequently accessed data on high-performance storage.

This strategy optimizes storage costs while maintaining acceptable performance.

Monitoring and performance analysis tools are crucial for evaluating file system performance.

These tools provide insights into file system usage, I/O patterns, and potential bottlenecks.

Administrators can use monitoring data to identify performance issues, optimize file system parameters, and make informed decisions about storage upgrades or capacity planning.

In summary, file system types and performance are essential considerations for system administrators and architects.

The choice of file system type should align with the specific use case and requirements of the system.

File system performance is influenced by factors such as storage media, configuration settings, workload characteristics, and advanced features.

Efficient file system management, including organization, tiering, and monitoring, is essential for achieving optimal performance and resource utilization.

Balancing data integrity, security, and performance is a continuous process that requires careful planning, tuning, and monitoring to ensure that the file system meets the needs of the computing environment.

## Chapter 6: CPU and Process Optimization

Memory is a vital resource in modern computer systems, playing a fundamental role in the execution of programs and the overall performance of the system.

Effective memory management is crucial for ensuring that the system operates efficiently, reliably, and securely.

Memory management involves the allocation, tracking, and optimization of memory resources to meet the demands of running processes and the operating system itself.

At its core, memory management revolves around the management of two primary types of memory: physical memory (RAM) and virtual memory.

Physical memory refers to the actual hardware memory modules installed in the computer, where data and programs are stored while they are actively being used.

Virtual memory, on the other hand, extends the physical memory by using a portion of the computer's storage device (usually a hard disk or SSD) to simulate additional memory.

This virtual memory space allows the system to run larger programs and handle more data than the physical memory alone would permit.

The operating system plays a central role in memory management, acting as the intermediary between processes and the physical and virtual memory resources.

One of the primary functions of the operating system's memory manager is to allocate and deallocate memory for processes as they are created and terminated.

Processes are individual program instances running on the computer, and each process requires memory for code, data, and temporary storage.

Memory allocation ensures that processes receive the memory they need to execute without interference from other processes, preventing memory conflicts.

Memory tracking involves keeping records of which memory blocks are in use, which are free, and which have been allocated to specific processes.

This tracking allows the operating system to efficiently allocate memory, avoid memory leaks, and release memory when it is no longer needed.

Processes communicate with the operating system's memory manager through a set of memory management functions and system calls.

For example, a process can request memory from the operating system when it needs to store data or execute code.

The memory manager evaluates these requests, allocates memory blocks, and returns references to the allocated memory back to the process.

When a process no longer requires a memory block, it can release it to the memory manager, making the memory available for other processes to use.

Memory optimization is another critical aspect of memory management.

Optimization techniques aim to improve memory usage and system performance by reducing fragmentation and maximizing the efficient use of memory resources.

Memory fragmentation occurs when memory becomes divided into small, non-contiguous blocks over time, making it challenging to allocate large, contiguous memory blocks for processes.

Operating systems use various techniques, such as memory compaction and defragmentation, to reduce fragmentation and ensure that memory is available for processes that require it.

Virtual memory is a key concept in modern memory management.

It allows the operating system to provide a uniform view of memory to processes, regardless of the physical memory available.

Virtual memory enables the illusion that a computer has more memory than it physically possesses, facilitating the execution of larger programs.

The concept of virtual memory involves mapping physical memory addresses to virtual memory addresses.

When a process accesses virtual memory, the operating system translates the virtual memory address to the corresponding physical memory address, ensuring that the correct data is retrieved or stored.

Virtual memory also provides a crucial feature known as memory protection.

Memory protection prevents processes from accessing or modifying memory that does not belong to them, enhancing system security and stability.

If a process attempts to access unauthorized memory, the operating system can terminate the offending process to prevent system corruption or data loss.

Memory management also includes techniques like memory paging and memory swapping.

Memory paging divides physical and virtual memory into fixed-size pages, simplifying memory allocation and management.

When physical memory becomes scarce, the operating system can move less frequently used pages to secondary storage (usually a hard disk or SSD) in a process called paging.

This frees up physical memory for processes that require it, but paging can introduce performance overhead due to the need to read and write data to secondary storage.

Memory swapping is a more aggressive technique that involves moving entire processes, including their code and data, to secondary storage when physical memory is exhausted.

Swapping allows the system to continue running, but it can significantly impact performance, as accessing data from secondary storage is much slower than accessing it from RAM.

Modern operating systems employ sophisticated memory management algorithms to balance memory allocation, tracking, optimization, and performance.

These algorithms aim to provide responsive and efficient memory management while minimizing overhead and resource contention.

Administrators and developers can also influence memory management through system configuration settings and memory allocation strategies.

In summary, memory management is a fundamental aspect of operating system functionality, responsible for allocating, tracking, and optimizing memory resources to ensure efficient and reliable system operation.

Effective memory management involves the allocation and deallocation of memory for processes, memory tracking, and optimization to reduce fragmentation and improve memory usage.

Virtual memory extends the capabilities of physical memory, allowing larger programs to run and providing memory protection.

Memory management techniques like paging and swapping help the operating system manage memory resources effectively, balancing the need for responsive performance and efficient memory usage.

Understanding memory management fundamentals is essential for system administrators, developers, and anyone involved in the design and maintenance of computer systems.

Central Processing Units (CPUs) are the heart of a computer system, responsible for executing instructions and running processes.

Effective CPU resource management is critical for ensuring that computer systems perform optimally and efficiently.

CPU resource management involves allocating, scheduling, and optimizing CPU resources to meet the demands of running processes and applications.

In modern computing environments, where multiple processes compete for CPU time, efficient management is essential.

One of the primary functions of the operating system is to allocate CPU time to processes.

Processes are individual program instances running on the computer, and each process requires CPU time to execute its instructions.

CPU allocation ensures that processes receive their fair share of CPU resources, preventing one process from monopolizing the CPU and causing performance degradation for others.

Processes communicate with the operating system's CPU scheduler, requesting CPU time when they are ready to execute.

The CPU scheduler evaluates these requests and determines the order in which processes are allowed to run on the CPU.

Scheduling algorithms play a crucial role in CPU resource management.

Different scheduling algorithms prioritize processes based on factors such as process priority, fairness, and responsiveness.

Round-robin scheduling, for example, allocates CPU time in a cyclic fashion, giving each process an equal share of CPU time.

Priority-based scheduling assigns CPU time based on the priority of the process, allowing higher-priority processes to run first.

Efficient CPU resource management requires balancing the competing goals of fairness, responsiveness, and system throughput.

Processes may have different levels of priority, reflecting their importance or resource requirements.

High-priority processes, such as real-time tasks, must receive CPU time promptly to meet their deadlines.

Lower-priority background tasks should not be starved of CPU time but may yield to higher-priority tasks when needed.

Efficiency in CPU resource management also involves minimizing context switches.

A context switch occurs when the CPU switches from running one process to another, requiring the operating system to save the state of the running process and load the state of the new process.

Context switches consume CPU resources and introduce overhead.

Efficient scheduling algorithms aim to reduce the frequency of context switches while ensuring that processes receive adequate CPU time.

In addition to process scheduling, CPU resource management encompasses techniques like load balancing.

Load balancing distributes CPU workloads evenly across multiple CPUs or CPU cores, ensuring that no CPU is heavily loaded while others are underutilized.

Load balancing techniques include task migration, where processes are moved between CPUs to achieve load balance, and task partitioning, where workloads are divided among multiple CPUs.

Load balancing enhances system performance, responsiveness, and resource utilization.

CPU resource management also involves managing interrupt handling.

Interrupts are signals that notify the CPU about events requiring immediate attention, such as hardware events or user input.

Efficient interrupt handling ensures that the CPU can respond promptly to interrupts without causing excessive delays to running processes.

Affinity management is another aspect of CPU resource management.

Affinity management allows processes to be bound or affinitized to specific CPUs or CPU cores.

This binding ensures that a process consistently runs on the same CPU, which can be beneficial for optimizing cache usage and reducing cache contention.

However, affinity management should be used judiciously, as it can impact load balancing and system responsiveness.

Efficient CPU resource management extends to power management as well.

Modern CPUs often support power-saving features, such as CPU frequency scaling (dynamic voltage and frequency scaling, DVFS), which allow the CPU to adjust its clock speed and power consumption based on workload demands.

Power management techniques aim to reduce energy consumption and heat generation while maintaining acceptable performance.

Administrators and system architects can configure power management policies to strike the right balance between performance and energy efficiency.

Monitoring and performance analysis tools are crucial for evaluating CPU resource management.

These tools provide insights into CPU usage, process execution times, context switches, and CPU load distribution.

Monitoring data helps administrators identify performance bottlenecks, tune scheduling parameters, and make informed decisions about system upgrades or capacity planning.

In summary, CPU resource management is a fundamental aspect of operating system functionality, responsible for allocating, scheduling, and optimizing CPU resources to ensure efficient and responsive system operation.

Efficient CPU resource management involves process scheduling, load balancing, interrupt handling, affinity management, and power management.

Scheduling algorithms aim to balance fairness, responsiveness, and system throughput, while load balancing enhances resource utilization and system performance.

Efficient CPU resource management is essential for achieving optimal system performance and responsiveness, particularly in multi-core and multi-processor environments.

## Chapter 7: Network Performance Tuning

Configuring and tuning a computer network is a critical task for system administrators and network engineers, as it directly impacts the performance, reliability, and security of networked systems.

Network configuration encompasses the setup and arrangement of network devices, protocols, and services to ensure effective communication.

Tuning involves optimizing network parameters, settings, and hardware to achieve desired performance levels.

Network configuration begins with the design and planning of the network topology.

The network topology defines how devices are connected and the physical or logical layout of the network.

Common network topologies include star, bus, ring, and mesh, each suitable for specific use cases and requirements.

Selecting the right network topology is crucial for achieving network efficiency and redundancy.

Network devices, such as routers, switches, and access points, play a pivotal role in network configuration.

Routers are responsible for routing data between different networks, ensuring that data packets reach their intended destinations.

Switches manage local network traffic by forwarding data only to the appropriate devices within a local area network (LAN).

Access points provide wireless connectivity for devices to connect to the network.

Properly configuring and securing these devices is essential for network integrity.

Network protocols are the rules and conventions that govern data communication across the network.

Common network protocols include TCP/IP, UDP, ICMP, and HTTP, each serving specific purposes.

TCP/IP, for example, is the foundation of the Internet and facilitates reliable data transmission.

UDP, on the other hand, is used for faster, connectionless communication.

ICMP handles error reporting and diagnostics, while HTTP is used for web browsing.

Configuring network protocols involves setting parameters, such as IP addresses, subnet masks, and port numbers, to enable communication between devices.

IP addressing is a critical aspect of network configuration, as it ensures that devices can be uniquely identified and located on the network.

IP addresses can be assigned statically or dynamically, depending on the network requirements.

Static IP addresses are manually assigned to devices and remain constant, while dynamic IP addresses are automatically assigned by a DHCP server.

Subnetting is a technique used to divide a large IP address space into smaller, manageable segments.

Subnetting enhances network security, simplifies management, and optimizes address allocation.

Routing is another essential component of network configuration, determining how data is forwarded between networks.

Routing protocols, such as OSPF and BGP, automate the process of finding the best path for data packets to reach their destinations.

Configuring routing protocols involves setting routing tables and policies to direct traffic efficiently.

Network services and applications, such as DNS, DHCP, and VPNs, provide additional functionality and connectivity to the network.

DNS (Domain Name System) translates human-readable domain names into IP addresses, facilitating web browsing and other network activities.

DHCP (Dynamic Host Configuration Protocol) automates the assignment of IP addresses to devices, simplifying network management.

VPNs (Virtual Private Networks) create secure, encrypted connections over public networks, enabling remote access and secure data transmission.

Network security is a paramount concern in network configuration.

Firewalls, intrusion detection systems (IDS), and encryption mechanisms are essential for safeguarding networked systems.

Firewalls filter network traffic based on predefined rules, allowing or blocking data packets based on criteria like source IP, destination port, and protocol.

Intrusion detection systems monitor network traffic for suspicious activity and alert administrators to potential security threats.

Encryption mechanisms, such as SSL/TLS, secure data in transit, ensuring that sensitive information remains confidential.

Quality of Service (QoS) is crucial for network configuration in environments where specific applications or services require prioritization.

QoS mechanisms allow administrators to allocate network resources to critical applications, ensuring that they receive sufficient bandwidth and low latency.

Network monitoring tools and protocols, like SNMP (Simple Network Management Protocol), are vital for assessing network performance and identifying issues.

SNMP enables the collection of data from network devices, helping administrators track network utilization, errors, and performance metrics.

Performance tuning involves optimizing network settings to improve throughput, reduce latency, and enhance overall network efficiency.

Bandwidth management, traffic shaping, and load balancing are common techniques used in network performance tuning.

Bandwidth management allocates available bandwidth to different types of traffic, ensuring that critical applications receive the necessary resources.

Traffic shaping controls the flow of network traffic, preventing congestion and prioritizing important data.

Load balancing distributes network traffic across multiple paths or devices, ensuring that no single component is overloaded.

Network security tuning involves configuring security policies, access control lists, and firewall rules to protect against threats and vulnerabilities.

Regularly updating and patching network devices and software is essential to address known security vulnerabilities.

Network configuration and tuning are ongoing processes, as network requirements evolve, and new technologies emerge.

Regular audits and assessments help ensure that network settings and configurations remain aligned with organizational goals.

In summary, network configuration and tuning are essential tasks for maintaining a robust, efficient, and secure network environment.

Properly configuring network devices, protocols, and services ensures that data flows smoothly and securely between devices.

Tuning network parameters and settings optimizes performance and enhances network reliability.

Network administrators and engineers must continuously monitor and adapt their network configurations to meet evolving requirements and address emerging challenges in the ever-changing landscape of network technology.

# Chapter 8: Storage Performance and RAID Configuration

Network throughput refers to the amount of data that can be transmitted through a network connection in a given time period.

Optimizing network throughput is essential for ensuring efficient data transfer, reduced latency, and improved overall network performance.

Several factors and strategies contribute to achieving optimal network throughput.

One fundamental aspect of optimizing network throughput is selecting the right network hardware.

Choosing high-quality network adapters, switches, routers, and cables can significantly impact the network's ability to transmit data efficiently.

Gigabit Ethernet and 10 Gigabit Ethernet technologies, for example, provide faster data transmission speeds compared to standard Ethernet connections.

Network administrators should consider the specific needs of their organization when selecting network hardware to ensure it can handle the expected workload.

Another critical factor in optimizing network throughput is minimizing network congestion.

Network congestion occurs when data traffic exceeds the network's capacity, leading to slowdowns and packet loss.

To reduce congestion, administrators can implement Quality of Service (QoS) policies that prioritize traffic for critical applications and allocate sufficient bandwidth to them.

Traffic shaping and bandwidth management tools can also help control the flow of data and prevent congestion.

Efficient routing is essential for optimizing network throughput.

Routing determines the path that data packets take from the source to the destination.

Implementing efficient routing protocols, such as Open Shortest Path First (OSPF) or Border Gateway Protocol (BGP), can ensure that data takes the shortest and fastest path to its destination.

Reducing the number of network hops and minimizing routing loops can improve network efficiency.

Network segmentation is another strategy for optimizing network throughput.

Dividing the network into smaller, isolated segments can help reduce broadcast traffic and improve data transfer speeds within each segment.

VLANs (Virtual Local Area Networks) are a common method for segmenting networks and enhancing throughput.

Optimizing the network's physical layout can also contribute to improved throughput.

Locating network devices strategically, minimizing cable lengths, and using high-quality cabling can reduce signal attenuation and electromagnetic interference, resulting in more reliable and faster data transmission.

Network monitoring and performance analysis tools are crucial for optimizing network throughput.

These tools provide insights into network traffic patterns, bandwidth utilization, and potential bottlenecks.

By analyzing this data, administrators can identify areas that require optimization and make informed decisions about network upgrades.

Efficiently handling network traffic at the transport layer is vital for optimizing throughput.

Transmission Control Protocol (TCP) is the most commonly used transport layer protocol, and it employs various mechanisms to ensure reliable data transmission.

TCP window scaling, for example, allows larger data windows, increasing the amount of data that can be in transit at any given time and improving throughput.

TCP/IP offload engines (TOEs) are hardware components that can accelerate TCP processing, further enhancing network performance.

Content delivery networks (CDNs) and edge computing are strategies for optimizing network throughput for web-based applications.

CDNs distribute content to geographically dispersed servers, reducing the distance data must travel to reach users and improving response times.

Edge computing places data processing closer to the source of data, reducing latency and improving application performance.

Optimizing network throughput also involves effective bandwidth management.

Bandwidth management tools enable administrators to allocate bandwidth based on application priorities, ensuring that critical applications receive the necessary resources for smooth operation.

Minimizing unnecessary traffic on the network can free up bandwidth for essential applications.

Implementing bandwidth caps, monitoring peer-to-peer file sharing, and using web filtering tools can help control and prioritize network traffic.

Load balancing is a technique used to distribute network traffic across multiple paths or devices.

Load balancers ensure that no single network component becomes overloaded, optimizing throughput and preventing bottlenecks.

Load balancing strategies may involve round-robin distribution, weighted distribution, or intelligent traffic routing based on server health and performance.

For organizations with remote or branch offices, Wide Area Network (WAN) optimization solutions can significantly improve network throughput.

WAN optimization appliances or software can compress data, reduce latency, and optimize traffic to enhance the performance of applications over long-distance connections.

Regularly updating and patching network equipment and software is crucial for optimizing network throughput.

Firmware updates and software patches often include performance improvements and security enhancements that can positively impact network performance.

In summary, optimizing network throughput is a multifaceted process that involves hardware selection, congestion management, efficient routing, network segmentation, physical layout optimization, monitoring and analysis, transport layer enhancements, content delivery strategies, bandwidth management, load balancing, WAN optimization, and regular maintenance.

By addressing these aspects comprehensively, network administrators and engineers can ensure that their networks perform at their best, delivering fast and reliable data transmission and supporting the needs of their organizations effectively.

## Chapter 9: Load Balancing and High Availability

Storage technologies play a pivotal role in modern computing environments, enabling data storage, retrieval, and management for a wide range of applications and purposes.

The choice of storage technology and configuration can significantly impact data availability, performance, and reliability.

One of the fundamental storage technologies is Hard Disk Drives (HDDs), which have been a staple of data storage for decades.

HDDs use spinning disks, known as platters, to store data magnetically and rely on mechanical read/write heads for data access.

Solid-State Drives (SSDs), on the other hand, have gained prominence due to their superior speed, durability, and energy efficiency.

SSDs use flash memory to store data, eliminating the moving parts found in HDDs.

This results in faster data access times and improved resistance to physical shocks.

Hybrid Drives combine the best of both worlds by incorporating a small SSD cache with a larger HDD for cost-effective storage with performance benefits.

Network-Attached Storage (NAS) and Storage Area Networks (SANs) are storage solutions that provide centralized storage resources for multiple devices or servers.

NAS devices are typically used for file-level storage and are connected to the network for shared access.

SANs, on the other hand, are designed for block-level storage and often employ dedicated high-speed networks for data access.

Direct-Attached Storage (DAS) is another storage solution where storage devices are directly connected to a single server or host.

DAS is commonly used when a single server requires exclusive access to the storage resources.

Storage technologies also include Optical Disc Drives (ODDs), which use laser technology to read and write data on optical discs such as CDs, DVDs, and Blu-ray discs.

While ODDs are less common for primary data storage today, they are still used for archival and backup purposes.

Redundant Array of Independent Disks (RAID) is a critical storage technology that enhances data redundancy, availability, and performance through disk array configurations.

RAID arrays combine multiple physical disks into a single logical unit, providing benefits such as data mirroring, striping, and parity.

RAID levels determine the specific configuration and redundancy features of the array.

RAID 0, for example, involves striping data across multiple disks, improving read/write performance but providing no redundancy.

RAID 1, in contrast, mirrors data across two or more disks, ensuring data availability even if one disk fails.

RAID 5 uses striping with distributed parity to provide a balance between performance and redundancy.

RAID 6 goes a step further by including dual parity, allowing for two disk failures without data loss.

RAID 10, also known as RAID 1+0, combines mirroring and striping for both redundancy and performance.

Storage technologies continue to evolve, with emerging technologies such as Non-Volatile Memory Express (NVMe) pushing the boundaries of storage speed and efficiency.

NVMe SSDs leverage the PCIe bus for ultra-fast data access, making them ideal for high-performance applications.

Storage technologies also include Cloud Storage, which enables data storage and retrieval through remote data centers and services provided by cloud providers like Amazon Web Services (AWS) and Microsoft Azure.

Cloud storage offers scalability, accessibility, and redundancy benefits, making it a popular choice for organizations seeking cost-effective and flexible storage solutions.

Software-Defined Storage (SDS) is a storage technology that abstracts and virtualizes storage resources, separating the management and control plane from the physical hardware.

SDS solutions offer flexibility and scalability, enabling organizations to manage storage resources more efficiently.

Storage technologies play a crucial role in data backup and recovery.

Backup solutions, such as tape drives, external hard drives, and cloud backups, help organizations protect their data from loss or corruption.

Data deduplication technologies reduce storage requirements by eliminating duplicate data in backup sets.

Storage technologies also extend to data archiving, which involves long-term storage of data that is no longer actively used but must be retained for legal, compliance, or historical purposes.

Archiving solutions ensure data integrity and accessibility over extended periods.

Data compression and encryption are essential storage technologies that help optimize storage capacity and protect sensitive data.

Data compression reduces the size of files or data streams, saving storage space and improving data transfer efficiency.

Data encryption ensures data security by converting information into a ciphertext that can only be decrypted with the appropriate encryption keys.

Storage technologies continue to advance, with innovations like Storage Class Memory (SCM) bridging the gap between traditional RAM and storage devices, providing low-latency, high-speed storage for critical workloads.

In-memory databases leverage SCM for near-instantaneous data access, benefiting applications that require real-time data processing.

Storage technologies also include hierarchical storage management (HSM) systems that automatically move data between different storage tiers based on access frequency and priority.

These systems optimize storage costs while maintaining data accessibility.

Data tiering and caching are techniques that enhance storage performance by placing frequently accessed data in high-speed storage layers, such as SSDs, while less frequently accessed data is stored on slower, more cost-effective storage media.

Storage technologies are critical components of the modern IT infrastructure, supporting various data-intensive applications and workloads.

The choice of storage technology and configuration should align with an organization's specific needs, balancing factors like performance, capacity, redundancy, and cost.

As storage technologies continue to evolve, staying informed about the latest advancements is essential for making informed decisions and optimizing data management strategies.

In summary, storage technologies encompass a wide range of hardware and software solutions that provide data storage, protection, and management capabilities.

From traditional HDDs to cutting-edge NVMe SSDs, storage technologies cater to diverse storage requirements and performance demands.

RAID configurations enhance data redundancy and availability, while cloud storage and SDS offer flexible and scalable storage options.

Data compression, encryption, and backup solutions ensure data integrity and security, while emerging technologies like SCM and in-memory databases drive innovation in the storage industry.

## Chapter 10: Scaling Infrastructure for Growth

Load balancing is a critical aspect of modern network and application architecture that plays a fundamental role in ensuring the availability, performance, and scalability of online services.

At its core, load balancing involves distributing network traffic or application requests across multiple servers or resources to prevent overloading and optimize resource utilization.

Load balancing is a fundamental concept in the realm of distributed computing, cloud computing, and web services.

The primary goal of load balancing is to ensure that no single server or resource becomes overwhelmed with traffic, thereby preventing performance degradation or downtime.

Load balancing strategies and techniques are employed in various scenarios, ranging from web applications and e-commerce platforms to data centers and cloud infrastructure.

One of the key motivations for load balancing is to achieve high availability.

By distributing traffic across multiple servers or resources, load balancing ensures that if one of them fails or experiences issues, the remaining ones can still handle incoming requests, minimizing service disruptions.

Load balancing also enhances fault tolerance, as it reduces the impact of hardware failures or software crashes on the overall system.

Scalability is another significant benefit of load balancing.

As traffic grows, organizations can add additional servers or resources to the load balancer pool, effectively scaling their infrastructure to accommodate increased demand.

Load balancing allows for dynamic resource allocation, ensuring that each server receives a manageable share of the traffic while maximizing the overall system's capacity.

There are various load balancing algorithms and strategies designed to achieve different objectives.

Round Robin is one of the simplest load balancing algorithms, where incoming requests are evenly distributed among the available servers in a circular manner.

While Round Robin is easy to implement and suitable for scenarios with homogeneous servers, it may not consider server load or performance.

Weighted Round Robin extends the basic Round Robin algorithm by assigning weights to each server, indicating its capacity or processing power.

Servers with higher weights receive more requests than those with lower weights, allowing for better resource allocation.

Least Connections is another load balancing algorithm that directs traffic to the server with the fewest active connections.

This approach aims to distribute the load more evenly based on the current state of the servers, which can be especially useful when servers have varying capacities or workloads.

IP Hash load balancing uses a hash function to map the client's IP address to a specific server.

This ensures that requests from the same client are consistently directed to the same server, which can be essential for maintaining session data or stateful connections.

Least Response Time load balancing considers the response times of servers when making routing decisions.

Requests are sent to the server with the shortest response time, which can lead to improved user experience and performance optimization.

Content-based load balancing takes into account the type or content of the incoming requests.

For example, requests for images or videos may be directed to specialized servers optimized for serving static content, while other requests go to application servers for dynamic content generation.

Geographic load balancing routes traffic based on the client's geographic location.

This strategy is useful for global organizations that want to ensure low-latency access to their services by directing users to the nearest data center or server location.

Health checks and monitoring are essential components of load balancing strategies.

Load balancers regularly check the health and availability of individual servers, ensuring that only healthy servers receive traffic.

When a server becomes unresponsive or experiences issues, the load balancer automatically redirects traffic to healthy servers, maintaining service continuity.

Load balancing can be implemented using both hardware and software solutions.

Hardware load balancers are dedicated devices designed for high-performance load balancing and often include advanced features such as SSL termination and content caching.

Software load balancers, on the other hand, are implemented as applications or services running on standard servers or virtual machines.

Software load balancers are more flexible and cost-effective, making them a popular choice in cloud environments and virtualized infrastructures.

Load balancing is not limited to web applications and HTTP traffic.

It can also be applied to other network services, such as DNS load balancing, where requests to domain names are distributed across multiple DNS servers to ensure redundancy and improved performance.

Load balancing strategies can be further enhanced by combining multiple algorithms or using adaptive load balancing techniques.

Adaptive load balancing involves continuously monitoring server performance and adjusting the routing of traffic in real-time based on various metrics such as server load, response times, and error rates.

Global Server Load Balancing (GSLB) extends load balancing across multiple data centers or cloud regions, allowing organizations to achieve high availability and disaster recovery capabilities on a global scale.

In summary, load balancing is a foundational concept in modern IT infrastructure that ensures the availability, performance, and scalability of networked services.

By distributing traffic across multiple servers or resources using various load balancing algorithms and strategies, organizations can achieve fault tolerance, optimize resource utilization, and enhance the user experience.

Whether implemented with hardware or software solutions, load balancing is a critical component of a resilient and high-performing network architecture.

## BOOK 4
## UNIX AND LINUX SYSTEM ADMINISTRATION HANDBOOK
## DEVOPS AND CONTINUOUS INTEGRATION/CONTINUOUS
## DEPLOYMENT (CI/CD)

### ROB BOTWRIGHT

# Chapter 1: Introduction to DevOps and CI/CD

Scalability is a fundamental concept in the world of technology and computing, essential for building systems and applications that can adapt to changing demands and grow with the needs of users.

Scalability is the ability of a system to handle increasing workloads and resource requirements without compromising performance, reliability, or quality of service.
It is a key consideration in designing and managing complex systems, from web applications and databases to cloud services and distributed computing environments.
Scalability principles guide the development and operation of scalable systems, helping organizations meet the challenges of a dynamic and ever-expanding digital landscape.

One of the core principles of scalability is the ability to add resources seamlessly.
In a scalable system, adding more servers, storage, or network capacity should not disrupt ongoing operations or require major architectural changes.
This principle ensures that as user traffic or data volume increases, the system can accommodate the growth by simply provisioning additional resources.
Scalability is closely tied to performance optimization.

Efficient resource utilization and performance tuning are essential to ensure that a system can handle increased workloads while maintaining acceptable response times.

This principle emphasizes the importance of identifying and eliminating bottlenecks, optimizing algorithms, and fine-tuning configurations to maximize performance.

Horizontal scalability, often referred to as "scaling out," is a key principle for many systems.

It involves adding more identical nodes or instances to a system to distribute the load and improve performance. Horizontal scalability is often associated with cloud-based solutions, where instances can be added or removed dynamically based on demand.

Vertical scalability, or "scaling up," is another principle that involves increasing the capacity of individual resources, such as upgrading a server with more CPU, memory, or storage.

While vertical scalability can provide a quick performance boost, it may have limitations in terms of cost and the ultimate capacity it can achieve.

Load balancing is a fundamental principle in achieving scalability.

Load balancers distribute incoming requests or traffic across multiple servers or resources, ensuring that no single resource becomes overwhelmed.

This principle helps in achieving fault tolerance, as well as efficient resource utilization.

Statelessness is a crucial concept for scalability in distributed systems.

Stateless systems do not store user-specific data or session information on individual servers.

Instead, they store such information in shared databases or use tokens to maintain user sessions.

This principle allows requests to be directed to any server, making it easier to scale horizontally without concerns about user data residing on a specific server.

Caching is an essential principle for improving scalability and performance.

By caching frequently accessed data, systems can reduce the need to fetch information from slower storage or databases, resulting in faster response times and reduced load on backend resources.

Distributed computing principles, such as microservices and containerization, play a significant role in achieving scalability.

Microservices architecture decomposes a complex application into smaller, independently deployable services, making it easier to scale individual components.

Containerization technologies like Docker enable the deployment of lightweight, isolated containers that can be easily scaled horizontally.

Auto-scaling is a key principle for achieving dynamic scalability.

Auto-scaling systems monitor resource utilization and automatically adjust the number of instances or resources based on predefined thresholds or policies.

This principle ensures that systems can adapt to fluctuating workloads without manual intervention.

Scalability principles also include data management strategies.

Distributed databases and data partitioning are used to distribute data across multiple servers or nodes, ensuring that data access remains efficient as the system scales.

Data sharding, replication, and NoSQL databases are common approaches to managing data in scalable systems.

Monitoring and analytics are crucial for maintaining scalability.

Effective monitoring tools and performance analytics help identify performance issues, resource bottlenecks, and anomalies in real-time, allowing for proactive adjustments and optimizations.

Scalability is not solely a technical concern; it also encompasses organizational and operational aspects.

Scalability planning involves forecasting future growth, defining scalability objectives, and establishing processes and procedures to support expansion.

Regular testing and capacity planning are essential to validate scalability assumptions and ensure that the system can handle anticipated workloads.

In summary, scalability principles are fundamental to building robust and adaptable systems that can meet the evolving needs of users and businesses.

By following these principles, organizations can design, implement, and operate systems that can scale seamlessly, maintain high performance, and provide a reliable and responsive user experience.

Scalability is not a one-time consideration but an ongoing commitment to ensuring that systems can grow and evolve with the ever-changing demands of the digital landscape.

## Chapter 2: Version Control with Git

DevOps is a philosophy and set of practices that bring together development (Dev) and operations (Ops) teams to collaborate throughout the software development lifecycle.

The DevOps approach aims to streamline and automate processes, reduce friction between teams, and deliver software more rapidly and reliably.

DevOps is built on several key principles that guide its practices and methodologies.

One of the fundamental principles of DevOps is the automation of manual tasks and processes.

By automating tasks such as code builds, testing, deployment, and configuration management, DevOps teams can reduce errors, increase efficiency, and accelerate the delivery of software.

Automation ensures consistency and repeatability in the software development and deployment process.

Another core principle of DevOps is continuous integration (CI), which involves frequently integrating code changes into a shared repository.

Each integration triggers an automated build and testing process to identify issues early in the development cycle.

Continuous integration encourages collaboration among developers and ensures that code changes are validated against the existing codebase.

Continuous delivery (CD) extends the CI concept by automating the deployment process.

In a continuous delivery pipeline, code changes that pass automated tests are automatically deployed to production or staging environments.

This principle allows for rapid and reliable software releases, reducing the time between code changes and delivery to end-users.

Continuous deployment takes CD a step further, automatically deploying code changes to production without manual intervention.

While not suitable for all organizations or applications, continuous deployment can enable extremely fast release cycles.

Infrastructure as code (IaC) is another fundamental principle of DevOps.

IaC involves defining and provisioning infrastructure (servers, networks, and storage) using code and automation tools.

This principle allows for consistent and repeatable infrastructure deployments, making it easier to manage and scale environments.

Monitoring and feedback are critical principles in DevOps.

Continuous monitoring of applications and infrastructure provides real-time visibility into system performance and helps detect and resolve issues proactively.

Feedback loops between development, operations, and end-users enable teams to gather insights and make data-driven decisions for improvements.

The principle of collaboration emphasizes breaking down silos between development and operations teams.

DevOps promotes a culture of shared responsibility and encourages cross-functional teams to work together seamlessly.

Collaboration fosters better communication, faster problem-solving, and improved overall efficiency.

Another key principle of DevOps is security.

Security should be integrated into every phase of the software development lifecycle, from design and coding to testing and deployment.

DevOps teams must consider security as a shared responsibility and implement security practices and controls to protect software and data.

Scalability and flexibility are important principles for DevOps infrastructure.

Systems and environments should be designed to scale horizontally and vertically to accommodate changing workloads and demands.

Flexibility enables organizations to adapt quickly to new requirements and technologies.

A focus on culture and continuous improvement is at the heart of DevOps.

DevOps teams should foster a culture of experimentation, learning, and adaptation.

Continuous improvement practices, such as retrospectives and post-incident reviews, help teams identify areas for enhancement and make iterative changes.

DevOps practices encompass several methodologies and tools that support its principles.

One of the core methodologies is agile development, which promotes iterative and incremental development with a focus on customer feedback and collaboration.

Agile methodologies, such as Scrum and Kanban, align well with DevOps practices.

Continuous integration tools, like Jenkins, Travis CI, and CircleCI, automate the build and testing processes, enabling rapid feedback and integration.

Configuration management tools, such as Ansible, Puppet, and Chef, automate the provisioning and management of infrastructure and applications.

Containerization technologies, like Docker, provide a consistent and portable environment for running applications, making it easier to deploy and scale.

Container orchestration platforms, such as Kubernetes, manage the deployment, scaling, and monitoring of containerized applications.

Monitoring and observability tools, such as Prometheus, Grafana, and ELK Stack, provide insights into system performance and allow for proactive issue detection and resolution.

Collaboration and communication tools, like Slack and Microsoft Teams, facilitate real-time communication and collaboration among DevOps teams.

Security tools, such as security scanning and vulnerability assessment tools, help identify and mitigate security risks in code and infrastructure.

DevOps practices are not limited to software development but can be applied to infrastructure management, known as Infrastructure as Code (IaC), and even extend to areas like data operations (DataOps) and machine learning operations (MLOps).

In summary, DevOps principles and practices are a foundational part of modern software development and operations.

By emphasizing automation, continuous integration and delivery, collaboration, security, and culture, DevOps helps organizations deliver software faster, more reliably, and with higher quality.

DevOps methodologies and tools enable teams to respond to changing business needs, reduce operational overhead, and continuously improve their processes and products.

As technology continues to evolve, DevOps will remain a vital approach for organizations looking to thrive in the digital age.

## Chapter 3: Building and Packaging Applications

Git is a distributed version control system that plays a pivotal role in modern software development, enabling teams to collaborate effectively, track changes, and manage their codebase efficiently.

At its core, Git is a tool that allows developers to track and record changes to their codebase over time.

One of the fundamental concepts in Git is the repository, which is essentially a project's folder that contains all the files, history, and information about the project.

Git repositories can be stored locally on a developer's machine or hosted on remote servers, providing a centralized location for collaboration.

A key concept in Git is version control, which means managing different versions of a project's codebase.

Version control allows developers to work on code changes independently and then merge those changes into a common codebase when they are ready.

In Git, each version of a project is referred to as a "commit," which represents a snapshot of the code at a specific point in time.

Developers can create new commits to record their changes and contributions to the project.

Git also provides branching and merging capabilities, which are essential for collaboration and code organization.

Branching allows developers to create separate lines of development, or branches, for different features or bug fixes.

Each branch is like an isolated workspace where changes can be made independently of the main codebase.

Merging, on the other hand, is the process of integrating changes from one branch into another.

This allows multiple developers to work on different features concurrently and then merge their changes into the main codebase when they are complete.

One of the core principles of Git is that it is a distributed version control system, which means that each developer has a complete copy of the repository on their local machine.

This provides several advantages, such as the ability to work offline, faster access to project history, and reduced dependence on a centralized server.

The distributed nature of Git also enhances collaboration, as developers can easily share their changes with others by pushing and pulling commits to and from remote repositories.

A critical aspect of Git is its flexibility in managing different workflows.

Git supports a variety of branching and merging strategies, such as feature branching, release branching, and Gitflow, which can be tailored to fit the specific needs of a project or team.

Another essential concept in Git is the commit message, which is a brief description of the changes made in a commit.

Writing clear and informative commit messages is crucial for understanding the history and purpose of each change, especially when collaborating with others.

Git also provides tools for reviewing and inspecting changes, such as "git diff" to see the differences between commits and "git log" to view the commit history.

These tools help developers understand the evolution of the codebase and identify issues or improvements.

Branches in Git can have different lifecycles, depending on their purpose.

Feature branches, for example, are short-lived branches created for specific features or bug fixes.

Once the work on a feature branch is complete and reviewed, it is typically merged into the main branch, such as "master" or "main."

Release branches are used to prepare and stabilize a version of the software for release.

They are created from the main branch and may receive bug fixes and minor updates before being merged back into the main branch.

The "git pull" command is used to fetch changes from a remote repository and integrate them into the local branch.

This ensures that a developer's local repository is up to date with the latest changes from the remote repository.

Git also provides conflict resolution tools in case multiple developers make conflicting changes to the same part of a file.

Conflicts can be resolved by manually editing the file to reconcile the differences or by using merge tools provided by Git.

Another useful concept in Git is tagging, which allows developers to mark specific commits as important milestones or releases.

Tags make it easy to reference specific versions of the codebase and are often used for creating stable release points.

Git hosting platforms, such as GitHub, GitLab, and Bitbucket, offer additional collaboration features like pull requests, code reviews, and issue tracking.

These platforms enhance the Git workflow by providing a centralized location for collaboration, communication, and project management.

In summary, Git is a powerful version control system that enables developers to manage and track changes in their codebase efficiently.

Key concepts like repositories, commits, branches, and merges form the foundation of Git's version control capabilities.

The distributed nature of Git allows for flexible collaboration and the ability to work offline.

Understanding Git's principles and workflow is essential for modern software development, as it empowers teams to work together seamlessly and maintain code quality throughout a project's lifecycle.

## Chapter 4: Automating Testing and Quality Assurance

Application build processes are a critical aspect of software development, responsible for transforming source code into executable applications or libraries.

These processes encompass a series of steps that compile, assemble, and package code, resulting in deployable artifacts that can run on various platforms.

Build processes are essential for ensuring that software is consistent, reproducible, and ready for deployment.

The first step in an application build process is compiling the source code.

Compilation is the process of translating human-readable source code into machine-executable code, typically in the form of binaries or intermediate code.

Compilers are responsible for parsing source code, checking for syntax errors, and generating output files that can be executed.

The compiled code may also include optimizations to improve performance and reduce resource consumption.

The choice of programming language and compiler depends on the specific project requirements and the target platform.

Once the source code is compiled, the next step in the build process is linking.

Linking is the process of combining multiple compiled files and libraries into a single executable or shared library.

Linkers resolve references between code modules, ensuring that functions and data are correctly connected.

Dynamic linking allows libraries to be loaded at runtime, reducing the size of the executable and enabling updates without recompilation.

Static linking, on the other hand, includes library code directly in the executable, resulting in a standalone binary.

Dependency management is a crucial aspect of build processes.

Dependencies are external libraries or components that the application relies on to function correctly.

Build tools often include mechanisms for specifying and managing dependencies, ensuring that the required libraries are available during the build.

Dependency management tools, such as package managers, simplify the process of downloading and including external libraries in the build.

Another important aspect of application build processes is resource management.

Resources, such as images, configuration files, and templates, need to be included in the build to ensure that the application runs correctly.

Build scripts or configuration files specify which resources to include and how to package them.

Resource compression and optimization may also be part of the build process to reduce the size of the final artifacts.

Build automation is a key practice in modern software development.

Automation tools, such as build systems and continuous integration (CI) servers, streamline and orchestrate the build process.

Build systems define the steps and dependencies required to build an application, making it easier to reproduce the process across different environments.

CI servers automatically trigger builds when changes are committed to version control repositories, ensuring that code changes are tested and built consistently.

Testing is an integral part of the application build process.

Unit tests, integration tests, and other forms of testing are executed to verify that the application behaves as expected and meets quality standards.

Automated testing frameworks and tools are often integrated into the build process, allowing for rapid feedback on code changes.

Continuous integration and continuous delivery (CI/CD) pipelines are widely used to automate testing and deployment as part of the build process.

A critical aspect of build processes is configuration management.

Configuration files and settings determine how the application behaves in different environments, such as development, testing, and production.

Managing configurations separately from the source code allows for flexibility and consistency when deploying applications to various environments.

Build processes may include steps to customize configurations for each deployment target.

Versioning and packaging are important considerations in build processes.

Version numbers and metadata help identify and track the different builds and releases of an application.

Packaging formats, such as executable installers, container images, or package archives, are used to distribute the application to end-users or deployment environments.

Documentation is often generated as part of the build process.

Documentation can include user manuals, API references, release notes, and other information that helps users and developers understand how to use and interact with the application.

Build tools and generators can automate the generation of documentation from source code comments and metadata.

Security is a critical concern in build processes.

The build environment should be secured to prevent unauthorized access or tampering.

Dependency scanning tools can help identify and remediate vulnerabilities in third-party libraries and components.

Security checks and tests, such as static code analysis and vulnerability scanning, can be integrated into the build process to identify security issues early.

Build artifact storage and distribution are final steps in the build process.

Artifacts, including compiled binaries, libraries, and documentation, need to be stored in a central repository or artifact manager.

Distribution mechanisms, such as package repositories, cloud storage, or content delivery networks, are used to make artifacts available for deployment.

In summary, application build processes are a crucial component of software development, responsible for compiling, linking, testing, and packaging code into deployable artifacts.

Modern build processes benefit from automation, dependency management, testing, and documentation generation.

They are essential for ensuring that software is consistent, reliable, and ready for deployment in various environments.

Efficient and well-organized build processes contribute to the success and maintainability of software projects, enabling developers to deliver high-quality applications to end-users.

**Chapter 5: CI/CD Pipelines with Jenkins**

Automated Testing Strategies
Automated testing is an integral part of modern software development, allowing teams to systematically validate code changes, ensure software quality, and accelerate the development process.
Automated testing refers to the use of automated scripts and tools to execute test cases, check software functionality, and report the results.
These tests can be run quickly and consistently, making them a valuable asset for software development teams.
One of the key benefits of automated testing is repeatability.
Automated test scripts can be executed as many times as needed, ensuring that code changes do not introduce new defects or regressions.
This repeatability is especially valuable in agile and continuous integration/continuous delivery (CI/CD) environments, where code changes are frequent.
Another advantage of automated testing is speed.
Automated tests can be executed much faster than manual tests, allowing for rapid feedback on code changes.
This speed enables developers to identify and fix issues early in the development process, reducing the cost of bug fixing.
Automated testing also contributes to software reliability.

By automating repetitive and time-consuming tests, teams can focus their manual testing efforts on more complex and exploratory testing, where human judgment is required.

This shift in focus enhances the overall quality of the software.

Test automation can cover various types of testing, including unit testing, integration testing, functional testing, regression testing, and performance testing.

Unit tests focus on individual components or functions of the software and validate their correctness in isolation.

Integration tests verify that different components or services work together as expected.

Functional tests assess whether the software meets its functional requirements, while regression tests ensure that new code changes do not break existing functionality.

Performance tests evaluate the software's performance, scalability, and response times under different conditions.

Automated testing frameworks and tools are essential for implementing an effective testing strategy.

These tools provide the infrastructure and utilities to create, run, and manage automated tests.

Common automated testing frameworks include JUnit, TestNG, NUnit, and pytest for unit testing, and tools like Selenium, Appium, and Cypress for functional testing.

Continuous integration and continuous delivery (CI/CD) pipelines play a crucial role in automated testing strategies.

CI/CD pipelines automate the building, testing, and deployment of code changes.

In a typical CI/CD pipeline, automated tests are integrated into the process, ensuring that code changes are tested automatically before being merged and deployed.

Test automation requires careful planning and design.

A well-defined testing strategy includes selecting the appropriate types of tests, defining test cases, creating automated test scripts, and establishing a test data strategy.

Test cases should cover both positive and negative scenarios, boundary cases, and edge cases to ensure comprehensive test coverage.

Test data should be carefully managed to provide the necessary inputs and conditions for testing.

Maintaining a clean and isolated test environment is essential to avoid interference between tests and to ensure consistent results.

Test automation also involves handling test failures gracefully.

When a test fails, it is crucial to capture detailed information about the failure, such as the test inputs, expected results, and actual results.

This information helps developers diagnose and fix issues quickly.

Test reporting and logging are essential components of automated testing.

Test reports provide a summary of test execution, including the number of tests passed, failed, and skipped.

Detailed logs and reports enable teams to investigate test failures and track test coverage over time.

Test automation is not without its challenges.

One common challenge is test maintenance.

As the software evolves, automated test scripts may need to be updated to reflect changes in the application's functionality.

Failure to maintain tests can lead to false positives or false negatives, reducing the trustworthiness of the automated testing suite.

Test flakiness, where tests produce inconsistent results, can also be a challenge.

Flaky tests can be caused by factors like timing issues, race conditions, or environmental inconsistencies.

Addressing test flakiness requires careful test design and robust test infrastructure.

Test data management can pose challenges as well.

Generating and managing test data that accurately represents real-world scenarios can be complex, particularly for applications with complex data dependencies.

Additionally, test environments must be set up and configured consistently to ensure reproducible results.

To address these challenges, it is essential to establish best practices and guidelines for automated testing within your organization.

Teams should prioritize the most critical tests for automation to maximize the benefits of test automation while minimizing maintenance efforts.

Continuous improvement and refactoring of test code are essential to keep automated tests effective and reliable.

Collaboration between development and testing teams is crucial for successful test automation.

Testers and developers should work together to define test cases, design test data, and review and maintain test scripts.

Automated testing is not a one-size-fits-all solution.

The choice of testing strategy, tools, and frameworks should align with the specific needs and goals of the project.

Some projects may benefit from a higher percentage of unit tests, while others may focus more on end-to-end functional testing.

Regardless of the approach, automated testing is a valuable practice that contributes to software quality, accelerates development cycles, and helps teams deliver reliable and robust software to end-users.

In summary, automated testing is an essential practice in modern software development, offering benefits such as repeatability, speed, and improved software quality.

Automated testing spans various types of testing, including unit, integration, functional, regression, and performance testing, each with its specific focus and purpose.

Effective automated testing requires careful planning, test case design, test data management, and test environment setup.

Test automation tools and continuous integration/continuous delivery (CI/CD) pipelines play a crucial role in executing and managing automated tests. Despite challenges such as test maintenance, test flakiness, and test data management, organizations can benefit greatly from a well-defined and continuously improved automated testing strategy.

## Chapter 6: Containerization with Docker and Podman

Jenkins Setup and Configuration

Setting up and configuring Jenkins is a fundamental step in establishing a continuous integration and continuous delivery (CI/CD) pipeline for your software development projects.

Jenkins is an open-source automation server that facilitates building, testing, and deploying code changes automatically.

It provides a wide range of plugins and integrations that can be tailored to meet your specific requirements.

Before diving into the details of Jenkins setup and configuration, it's essential to understand the high-level objectives and components involved.

The primary goals of setting up Jenkins are to automate repetitive tasks, improve code quality through automated testing, and streamline the software delivery process.

Jenkins accomplishes these objectives by creating a pipeline of automated jobs that are triggered by code changes in version control repositories.

The Jenkins pipeline consists of multiple stages, such as building, testing, and deployment, each with its set of tasks and actions.

To begin the setup, you need to install Jenkins on a server or a machine where it will run.

Jenkins can be installed on various operating systems, including Windows, Linux, and macOS.

Once Jenkins is installed, it runs as a service, making it accessible via a web interface.

You can access the Jenkins web interface by opening a web browser and navigating to the URL where Jenkins is running, typically http://localhost:8080 if Jenkins is running on the same machine as your web browser.

The initial setup process involves unlocking Jenkins, which requires you to retrieve the administrator password from the server's filesystem.

The administrator password is stored in a file named "initialAdminPassword," typically found in the Jenkins installation directory.

After unlocking Jenkins, you can install additional plugins and customize its configuration.

Jenkins plugins are extensions that add functionality to Jenkins, such as integrating with version control systems, build tools, and deployment platforms.

The Jenkins Plugin Manager allows you to browse and install plugins from the Jenkins plugin repository.

Selecting the right plugins is essential for tailoring Jenkins to your project's needs.

Commonly used plugins include those for Git integration, Maven or Gradle build tools, and Docker support.

Once the desired plugins are installed, you can configure global settings in Jenkins, such as system properties, security options, and email notification settings.

Security settings are crucial for controlling user access and permissions within Jenkins.

You can define user accounts, assign roles, and configure authorization strategies to ensure that only authorized users can access Jenkins and perform specific actions.

Securing Jenkins is vital to protect sensitive project information and prevent unauthorized access.

With Jenkins set up and configured at a high level, the next step is to create a Jenkins job or pipeline that automates your software development workflow.

Jenkins jobs are defined using the Jenkins Domain Specific Language (DSL) or by using the Jenkins Pipeline plugin, which allows you to define build and deployment workflows as code.

Pipeline as Code (Jenkinsfile) provides a structured and version-controlled approach to defining your CI/CD pipeline.

In a Jenkinsfile, you can specify stages, steps, and post-build actions that Jenkins should execute when triggered by code changes.

For example, a Jenkinsfile might include stages for building the application, running unit tests, deploying to a staging environment, and promoting to production.

Each stage can have its set of configuration options and dependencies.

Jenkins also provides the flexibility to set up freestyle projects, which are graphical representations of build jobs that can be configured through the Jenkins web interface.

Freestyle projects are suitable for simpler build and deployment tasks.

Once your Jenkins job or pipeline is defined, you can configure the triggers that initiate the automation process.

Triggers can include code commits to a version control repository, scheduled builds, or manual initiation.

For example, you can set up Jenkins to automatically build and test your application whenever changes are pushed to the project's Git repository.

After configuring the triggers, it's essential to define the build environment, which includes specifying the build tools, dependencies, and build agents.

Build agents, also known as build slaves, are machines that execute the build jobs defined in Jenkins.

You can set up build agents on different machines or use cloud-based services to provide additional computing resources for your builds.

Once your Jenkins job or pipeline is set up and configured, you can run and monitor the automation process.

Jenkins provides a web-based dashboard that displays information about ongoing builds, completed builds, and build history.

The dashboard also shows the status of each build job, including whether the build succeeded or failed.

If a build job fails, Jenkins provides detailed logs and reports to help you diagnose and fix issues.

Monitoring and debugging build failures are essential for maintaining the reliability of your CI/CD pipeline.

Jenkins also supports parallel and distributed builds, allowing you to speed up the build process by running multiple build jobs concurrently.

Distributed builds can be set up to utilize multiple build agents, distributing the workload across multiple machines for increased efficiency.

To summarize, setting up and configuring Jenkins is a critical step in establishing an effective CI/CD pipeline for your software development projects.

It involves installing Jenkins, customizing its configuration, installing plugins, and defining Jenkins jobs or pipelines.

Security settings are crucial for controlling user access and permissions, and triggers are configured to initiate the automation process.

Build environments, including build tools and build agents, are defined, and the Jenkins dashboard is used to monitor and manage the CI/CD pipeline.

Jenkins offers flexibility and extensibility, making it a powerful automation tool for modern software development teams.

## Chapter 7: Orchestration with Kubernetes

Containers have revolutionized the way software is developed, deployed, and managed in recent years.

They offer a lightweight and efficient way to package and distribute applications, making it easier to build, ship, and run software across different environments.

At the heart of this containerization revolution is Docker, a popular platform for creating and managing containers.

In this chapter, we'll explore the fundamental concepts of containers, delve into the world of Docker, and understand why containers have become a game-changer in the world of software development.

Containers are a form of virtualization technology that allows you to package an application and all its dependencies into a single, portable unit called a container.

Unlike traditional virtualization, which runs multiple virtual machines (VMs) on a single physical server, containers share the host operating system's kernel, resulting in a smaller footprint and faster startup times.

Containers are isolated from each other, providing a level of security and resource management.

The concept of containerization dates back to the early 2000s, but it gained widespread adoption with the introduction of Docker in 2013.

Docker simplified the process of creating, distributing, and running containers, making container technology accessible to developers and organizations of all sizes.

Containers offer several benefits, including consistency across environments.

With containers, you can be confident that the application you develop and test on your local machine will behave the same way in production.

This consistency eliminates the dreaded "it works on my machine" problem that often plagues software development teams.

Containers also enable rapid scaling and resource optimization.

You can quickly spin up additional containers to handle increased traffic or workloads, and just as easily scale down when demand decreases.

This flexibility makes containers well-suited for microservices architectures and cloud-native applications.

Another advantage of containers is their portability.

A containerized application and its dependencies are bundled into a single image that can be easily shared and deployed across different environments, from development and testing to staging and production.

This portability simplifies the process of migrating applications to new infrastructure or cloud providers.

Docker, the most well-known container platform, plays a pivotal role in the containerization ecosystem.

Docker provides tools for creating, managing, and orchestrating containers.

At the core of Docker is the Docker Engine, which is responsible for running containers on a host system.

The Docker CLI (Command Line Interface) allows developers to interact with Docker and perform tasks like building, running, and managing containers.

Docker Hub is a cloud-based registry where you can find pre-built Docker images, share your own images, and collaborate with the Docker community.

Docker Compose is a tool for defining and running multi-container applications using a simple YAML file.

Docker Swarm and Kubernetes are popular orchestration tools that help manage and scale containerized applications in production environments.

To get started with Docker, you'll need to install Docker on your development machine or server.

Docker provides installation packages for various operating systems, including Windows, macOS, and various flavors of Linux.

Once Docker is installed, you can use the Docker CLI to pull, build, and run containers.

The Docker CLI syntax is straightforward and follows a common pattern: **docker [command] [options] [arguments]**.

For example, you can use **docker run** to start a container, **docker build** to create a custom container image, and **docker push** to upload images to Docker Hub.

Docker images are the building blocks of containers.

An image is a lightweight, standalone, executable package that includes everything needed to run a piece of software, including the code, runtime, system tools, libraries, and settings.

Images are created from a set of instructions called a Dockerfile, which specifies the base image, application code, and configuration.

Once an image is built, it can be used to create one or more containers.

Containers are instances of images that can be run as isolated processes on a host system.

Containers are defined by their image, and you can create multiple containers from the same image.

Containers have their file system, network, and process namespace, providing process isolation and ensuring that each container operates independently.

Docker images are typically hosted on Docker Hub, a public registry of container images, but you can also create and use private registries to store and share images within your organization.

When working with Docker, it's essential to understand the concept of a Dockerfile.

A Dockerfile is a plain-text configuration file that defines the steps required to build a Docker image.

It starts with a base image, often an official image from Docker Hub, and then specifies additional instructions to customize the image for your application.

These instructions can include copying files into the image, running commands to install software, and setting environment variables.

By following the instructions in the Dockerfile, you can create a reproducible and version-controlled process for building images.

Once you have a Dockerfile, you can use the **docker build** command to create an image from it.

The **docker build** command reads the Dockerfile, executes each instruction, and generates a new image.

Images are stored locally on your system and can be reused to create multiple containers.

To run a container from an image, you use the **docker run** command, which starts a new container instance based on the specified image.

You can also use the **-d** flag to run a container in the background and the **-p** flag to map ports between the container and the host system.

Containers can communicate with each other and the host system using a network bridge or other networking modes defined in Docker.

Docker also provides a feature called Docker Compose, which allows you to define and run multi-container applications using a single YAML file.

With Docker Compose, you can specify the services, networks, and volumes required for your application, making it easy to manage complex applications with multiple containers.

Docker has a rich ecosystem of official and community-contributed images available on Docker Hub.

Official images are curated and maintained by Docker, ensuring a high level of quality and security.

Community-contributed images are created by the Docker community and cover a wide range of software and applications.

When using images from Docker Hub, it's important to choose trusted sources and regularly update your images to include security patches and updates.

Docker's containerization technology has transformed the way software is developed, tested, and deployed.

Containers offer a lightweight, consistent, and portable way to package and distribute applications, making it easier to manage complex software systems.

Docker, as a leading container platform, simplifies the process of creating, running, and orchestrating containers.

Understanding the fundamentals of containers and Docker is essential for modern software development and deployment practices.

In the next chapters, we will dive deeper into Docker's features, best practices, and use cases, empowering you to leverage containerization effectively in your projects.

## Chapter 8: Configuration Management with Ansible

Kubernetes, often abbreviated as K8s, is an open-source container orchestration platform that has gained immense popularity in the world of cloud-native application deployment.

It was originally developed by Google and is now maintained by the Cloud Native Computing Foundation (CNCF).

Kubernetes provides a powerful and flexible framework for automating the deployment, scaling, and management of containerized applications.

At its core, Kubernetes is designed to abstract away the underlying infrastructure and provide a consistent way to deploy and manage applications across various environments, whether on-premises or in the cloud.

The fundamental concept in Kubernetes is the container, which is a lightweight, standalone executable package that includes everything needed to run an application, including code, runtime, libraries, and dependencies.

Kubernetes extends the concept of containers by allowing you to group them into pods, which are the smallest deployable units in Kubernetes.

A pod can contain one or more containers that share the same network namespace and storage volumes, making it easier to manage related processes together.

One of the key strengths of Kubernetes is its ability to handle container orchestration seamlessly.

This means that Kubernetes can automatically distribute containers across a cluster of machines, ensuring high availability and resource optimization.

Kubernetes provides a powerful scheduling mechanism that determines where containers should run based on resource requirements, constraints, and affinity rules.

Another critical aspect of Kubernetes is its self-healing capability.

If a container or pod fails, Kubernetes can automatically restart it on the same or another node in the cluster, ensuring that applications remain available and resilient.

Kubernetes also supports scaling applications horizontally by adding or removing pod replicas based on metrics or user-defined rules.

This autoscaling feature allows applications to handle varying workloads efficiently.

To manage containers and pods, Kubernetes introduces several essential components.

The Control Plane, also known as the Kubernetes Master, consists of the API Server, etcd, the Controller Manager, and the Scheduler.

The API Server acts as the front-end for the Kubernetes control plane, exposing the Kubernetes API, which users and administrators interact with.

etcd is a distributed key-value store that stores the configuration data and state of the entire cluster.

The Controller Manager enforces desired state, such as maintaining the correct number of replicas for a pod or updating a service's load balancer configuration.

The Scheduler is responsible for placing pods on suitable nodes based on various factors, including resource requirements and affinity rules.

On each node in the cluster, there is the Kubelet, which communicates with the API Server and ensures that containers are running in pods as expected.

Container runtimes, such as Docker or containerd, are responsible for actually running the containers inside pods.

Additionally, the Kube Proxy manages network communication between pods and external services, allowing them to discover and communicate with each other.

Kubernetes organizes applications using higher-level abstractions, including Deployments, Services, and ConfigMaps.

Deployments describe the desired state of an application, including the number of replicas and the container image to use.

Kubernetes ensures that the actual state matches the desired state, automatically scaling, rolling out updates, and rolling back changes as needed.

Services define a logical set of pods and a policy for accessing them.

They provide a stable IP address and DNS name for accessing pods, allowing applications to discover and communicate with each other without needing to know their exact network locations.

ConfigMaps store configuration data that can be mounted as files or passed as environment variables to containers.

This separation of configuration from application code makes it easier to manage and update configurations independently.

Kubernetes also supports Secrets, which are used to store sensitive information like passwords and API keys securely.

Kubernetes is highly extensible, with a rich ecosystem of extensions and add-ons.

These include Helm, a package manager for Kubernetes, which simplifies the deployment and management of complex applications.

Monitoring and logging solutions like Prometheus and Grafana help you gain insights into the health and performance of your cluster and applications.

Ingress controllers enable the management of external access to services within the cluster.

Kubernetes also integrates with continuous integration and continuous delivery (CI/CD) tools, allowing you to automate the deployment of your applications.

One of the notable features of Kubernetes is its ability to run across multiple cloud providers or on-premises data centers using the same set of APIs and tools.

This portability allows organizations to avoid vendor lock-in and choose the infrastructure that best suits their needs.

Kubernetes is also designed to be highly available and resilient, with built-in mechanisms for failover and disaster recovery.

This ensures that your applications remain accessible and operational even in the face of hardware or network failures.

Kubernetes has a vibrant and active community that continually develops new features, extensions, and best practices.

It's essential to keep up with these advancements to take full advantage of Kubernetes in your projects.

As you dive deeper into Kubernetes, you'll explore advanced topics such as custom resource definitions (CRDs) for extending the Kubernetes API, role-based access control (RBAC) for fine-grained authorization, and network policies for controlling pod-to-pod communication.

In summary, Kubernetes is a powerful container orchestration platform that abstracts away the complexities of infrastructure management, making it easier to deploy, scale, and manage containerized applications.

Understanding its fundamental concepts and components is crucial for harnessing its full potential and building robust, cloud-native applications.

**Chapter 9: Monitoring and Logging in DevOps**

Effective monitoring of both infrastructure and applications is essential for ensuring the reliability, performance, and security of your IT systems.

Monitoring provides real-time insights into the health and behavior of your systems, allowing you to proactively identify and address issues before they impact your users or business operations.

In this chapter, we'll explore the importance of monitoring, the key components of a monitoring system, and best practices for implementing monitoring in your organization.

Monitoring serves as a critical component of IT operations, providing visibility into the various layers of your infrastructure and applications.

Without monitoring, it's challenging to detect and diagnose problems, leading to increased downtime, decreased user satisfaction, and potential revenue loss.

Monitoring helps you answer essential questions like "Is my system performing well?", "Are there any anomalies or errors?", and "How can I optimize resource utilization?"

In the realm of infrastructure monitoring, the focus is on tracking the health and performance of physical and virtual components such as servers, network devices, storage, and databases.

Infrastructure monitoring aims to provide a holistic view of the underlying systems that support your applications.

On the other hand, application monitoring is concerned with understanding how your software behaves from the end-user's perspective.

This includes monitoring the responsiveness and availability of web applications, APIs, and services, as well as tracking error rates and latency.

Application monitoring allows you to pinpoint issues that may arise within your code, database queries, or third-party integrations.

A well-rounded monitoring strategy should encompass both infrastructure and application monitoring to provide a complete picture of system health.

Modern monitoring systems leverage a variety of data sources and techniques to collect and analyze data.

One common approach is to use agents or collectors that run on monitored servers and gather metrics and logs.

These agents transmit data to a central monitoring server or cloud-based service for processing and analysis.

In addition to agent-based monitoring, you can also collect data from various sources, including system logs, APIs, and external services.

The choice of data collection method depends on your specific requirements and the technologies used in your environment.

Once data is collected, it is stored in a time-series database that allows for efficient querying and visualization of historical and real-time data.

Prometheus and InfluxDB are popular open-source time-series databases used in many monitoring setups.

Effective monitoring also involves the use of dashboards and visualization tools to display relevant data in a user-friendly format.

These dashboards provide a quick overview of system health and performance and allow operators to drill down into specific metrics when investigating issues.

Popular visualization tools for monitoring include Grafana and Kibana.

Alerting is another critical aspect of monitoring, as it enables you to be proactive in responding to issues.

Alerts are triggered based on predefined conditions and thresholds, such as CPU usage exceeding a certain percentage or the number of error logs reaching a specified count.

When an alert is triggered, it can notify administrators or operations teams through various channels, including email, SMS, or integration with incident management systems like PagerDuty or Opsgenie.

To ensure that monitoring remains effective, it's essential to establish clear and well-defined alerting policies.

These policies should include the severity of alerts, escalation procedures, and on-call rotations to ensure that the right people are notified at the right time.

Anomaly detection is an advanced monitoring technique that can identify unusual patterns or deviations from expected behavior.

Machine learning algorithms can be applied to historical data to establish baseline behavior and automatically detect anomalies.

Anomaly detection can be particularly valuable in complex and dynamic environments where traditional threshold-based alerting may not be sufficient.

As part of your monitoring strategy, you should also consider the retention and archiving of monitoring data. Decide how long you need to retain historical data for analysis and compliance purposes, and implement data retention policies accordingly.

In some cases, it may be necessary to archive data to long-term storage solutions for regulatory compliance.

Security is a crucial aspect of monitoring infrastructure and applications.

Ensure that your monitoring system is protected from unauthorized access, and consider encrypting data in transit and at rest.

Regularly review access controls and audit logs to detect any suspicious activities related to your monitoring infrastructure.

It's also essential to monitor the monitoring system itself to ensure its availability and performance.

Implement monitoring checks that verify the health of your monitoring infrastructure, such as the status of data collectors, alerting components, and dashboard services.

Cloud-based monitoring services, such as Amazon CloudWatch or Azure Monitor, offer scalable and integrated solutions for monitoring resources and applications hosted in cloud environments.

These services provide preconfigured metrics and dashboards for popular cloud services and allow you to create custom monitoring solutions tailored to your specific needs.

When setting up a monitoring system, consider the scalability and growth of your infrastructure and applications.

Ensure that your monitoring solution can handle an increasing volume of data and resources as your organization grows.

This may involve deploying additional monitoring agents, scaling your time-series database, or using distributed monitoring architectures.

Effective monitoring requires continuous improvement and optimization.

Regularly review and refine your monitoring policies, alerts, and dashboards to adapt to changing requirements and priorities.

Consider conducting post-mortem analysis of incidents to identify areas where monitoring can be enhanced to prevent similar issues in the future.

Collaboration and communication are essential aspects of monitoring.

Ensure that your monitoring data is accessible to all relevant teams, including operations, development, and security.

Collaborative dashboards and incident management platforms can facilitate communication and coordination when addressing issues.

In summary, monitoring infrastructure and applications is a critical practice for maintaining the reliability and performance of your IT systems.

A comprehensive monitoring strategy should encompass both infrastructure and application monitoring, leveraging a variety of data sources and techniques.

Effective monitoring involves data collection, storage, visualization, alerting, and anomaly detection.

Security considerations should be integrated into your monitoring practices to protect sensitive data and ensure the integrity of your monitoring infrastructure.

Continuous improvement and collaboration are key to maintaining an effective monitoring system that can adapt to the evolving needs of your organization.

## Chapter 10: DevSecOps and Security Automation

DevSecOps is a cultural and technical movement that aims to integrate security practices into the DevOps workflow.

It recognizes the need to shift security left in the software development process, meaning that security is considered from the very beginning of a project.

The traditional approach to security, where it's a separate phase that occurs after development, is no longer sufficient in today's fast-paced, agile software development environments.

In DevSecOps, security becomes an integral part of the entire software development lifecycle.

The core principle of DevSecOps is that security should be everyone's responsibility, not just the job of a dedicated security team.

Developers, operations teams, and security professionals must collaborate closely to build and maintain secure systems.

This collaboration starts with a shared understanding of security requirements and risks.

Security should be treated as a feature, and its requirements should be defined alongside other functional and non-functional requirements.

Security should not be seen as a blocker but as an enabler of the development process.

DevSecOps encourages the use of security as code, where security policies and controls are codified and automated.

This includes defining security checks, such as vulnerability scanning and compliance checks, as code that can be incorporated into the CI/CD pipeline.

Automating security checks ensures that security is consistently applied and that vulnerabilities are identified early in the development process.

Shift-left testing is a key practice in DevSecOps, where security testing is performed as early as possible in the development cycle.

This includes static code analysis, dynamic application security testing (DAST), and interactive application security testing (IAST).

By identifying and fixing security issues early, the cost and effort required for remediation are significantly reduced.

Another critical practice in DevSecOps is the use of containerization and container orchestration platforms like Docker and Kubernetes.

Containers provide a way to package applications and their dependencies in a consistent and isolated environment.

DevSecOps teams can define security policies for container images and ensure that these policies are enforced as part of the CI/CD pipeline.

Containers also facilitate microservices architecture, which can improve security by isolating components and limiting the blast radius of potential security incidents.

Infrastructure as code (IaC) is a fundamental component of DevSecOps.

IaC allows infrastructure to be defined and provisioned through code, enabling consistent and repeatable deployments.

Security policies can be applied to IaC scripts to ensure that infrastructure is configured securely.

Automated tools can assess IaC code for security vulnerabilities and compliance with security policies.

Immutable infrastructure, where servers and infrastructure components are not modified after deployment, is a concept closely aligned with DevSecOps.

Immutable infrastructure reduces the attack surface by ensuring that only trusted, preconfigured images are used.

In case of security vulnerabilities or configuration issues, new images can be created and deployed, eliminating the need for patching and reducing the window of exposure.

Continuous monitoring and threat detection are essential practices in DevSecOps.

Security teams should have visibility into the production environment and be alerted to suspicious activities or potential security incidents.

Security information and event management (SIEM) systems and intrusion detection systems (IDS) play a crucial role in monitoring for security threats.

Security incidents should be treated as incidents, and incident response plans should be well-defined and tested regularly.

The concept of chaos engineering, which involves intentionally causing failures in a controlled environment, can be used to assess an organization's readiness to respond to security incidents.

DevSecOps also emphasizes the importance of security awareness and training for all team members.

Developers should be educated about secure coding practices, and operations teams should understand the security implications of their configurations.

Security professionals should stay up-to-date with the latest threats and vulnerabilities.

DevSecOps encourages a shift from a reactive security posture to a proactive and preventative one.

This means that security teams work closely with development and operations to identify and mitigate security risks before they are exploited by attackers.

Threat modeling is a technique used to assess the potential threats and vulnerabilities of a system.

By identifying and prioritizing threats, teams can focus their efforts on addressing the most critical risks.

DevSecOps encourages the use of threat modeling as a proactive approach to security.

Compliance is another aspect of DevSecOps, as organizations must adhere to regulatory requirements and industry standards.

Automated compliance checks can be integrated into the CI/CD pipeline to ensure that deployments meet necessary compliance standards.

DevSecOps also emphasizes the importance of security testing in the context of continuous integration and continuous delivery (CI/CD).

Security testing should be automated and integrated into the CI/CD pipeline to provide rapid feedback to developers.

Static code analysis tools can identify potential vulnerabilities in the source code, while dynamic testing tools can assess the security of running applications.

DevSecOps recognizes that security is not a one-time effort but an ongoing process.

Organizations should continuously monitor and assess their security posture, adapt to new threats, and evolve their security practices.

Collaboration and communication are crucial in DevSecOps, as teams with different expertise must work together effectively.

Security teams should provide guidance and support to development and operations teams, rather than acting as gatekeepers.

In summary, DevSecOps is a holistic approach to integrating security into the software development lifecycle.

It emphasizes collaboration, automation, and a proactive mindset to ensure that security is not an afterthought but an integral part of delivering secure and reliable software.

In today's fast-paced software development landscape, continuous integration and continuous delivery (CI/CD) pipelines have become the backbone of efficient and agile software delivery.

These pipelines automate the process of building, testing, and deploying software, enabling organizations to release updates rapidly and consistently.

However, with the increasing frequency of software releases, the need for robust security practices has never been more critical.

Integrating security into CI/CD pipelines is essential for identifying and mitigating vulnerabilities early in the development process.

This chapter explores the principles and practices of integrating security into CI/CD pipelines to ensure that software is not only delivered quickly but also securely.

Traditionally, security assessments and checks have been separate phases that occurred after development and before production deployment.

This approach often resulted in delays as security teams conducted manual assessments and developers made remediations.

In contrast, the DevSecOps philosophy promotes shifting security left, which means addressing security concerns as early as possible in the software development lifecycle.

Integrating security into CI/CD pipelines is a key aspect of implementing DevSecOps practices.

One of the fundamental principles of integrating security into CI/CD pipelines is to automate security checks.

This automation ensures that security assessments are consistently applied to every code change and software build.

Automated security checks include static code analysis, dynamic application security testing (DAST), software composition analysis (SCA), and more.

Static code analysis tools scan the source code for known vulnerabilities, coding errors, and security weaknesses.

By automating static code analysis as part of the CI/CD pipeline, developers receive immediate feedback on potential security issues as they write code.

Dynamic application security testing, on the other hand, assesses the running application for vulnerabilities by simulating real-world attacks.

Integrating DAST into the CI/CD pipeline helps identify runtime vulnerabilities that may not be apparent through static analysis alone.

Software composition analysis tools scan for known vulnerabilities in third-party libraries and dependencies, helping organizations avoid using components with known security flaws.

Another critical aspect of integrating security into CI/CD pipelines is the use of security as code.

Security as code means codifying security policies, configurations, and controls.

This allows organizations to define security requirements as code and automate their enforcement in the CI/CD pipeline.

For example, organizations can codify security policies related to authentication, authorization, data encryption, and network segmentation.

These policies can then be automatically checked during the deployment process, ensuring that security controls are consistently applied.

Containerization, which is commonly used in modern CI/CD pipelines, introduces new security considerations.

Containers package applications and their dependencies, creating isolated environments that run consistently across different environments.

However, without proper security measures, containers can introduce security risks.

Integrating container security into CI/CD pipelines involves scanning container images for vulnerabilities, adhering to container security best practices, and monitoring container behavior in runtime environments.

Container security tools and practices should be integrated into the CI/CD pipeline to ensure that containerized applications are secure from the start.

Security gates are another essential component of integrating security into CI/CD pipelines.

Security gates are automated checkpoints in the pipeline that assess the security of the software being deployed.

These gates can include vulnerability scanning, compliance checks, and security testing.

If a security gate identifies issues that do not meet the organization's security policies, the deployment process is halted, and the issues must be addressed before proceeding.

Security gates help enforce security standards and prevent insecure code from reaching production environments.

Another best practice is to leverage infrastructure as code (IaC) for provisioning and configuring infrastructure.

IaC allows organizations to define infrastructure resources, such as servers, networks, and security groups, as code.

By integrating IaC into the CI/CD pipeline, infrastructure can be consistently and securely provisioned for each deployment.

This approach reduces the risk of misconfigurations and ensures that infrastructure is compliant with security policies.

Shift-left security testing is a cornerstone of integrating security into CI/CD pipelines.

By shifting security testing to the earliest stages of development, organizations can identify and remediate vulnerabilities before they propagate into production.

Security testing includes both automated scanning and manual testing by security professionals.

Additionally, organizations can employ threat modeling to assess potential security threats and risks during the design phase of a project.

This proactive approach helps developers and security teams work together to address security concerns from the outset.

Integrating security into CI/CD pipelines also extends to access control and permissions.

Organizations should implement role-based access control (RBAC) and enforce the principle of least privilege (PoLP) to ensure that only authorized individuals have access to critical systems and resources.

Access control policies and permissions should be codified and validated as part of the CI/CD pipeline.

Finally, organizations should maintain a security mindset throughout the CI/CD process.

Security should not be viewed as a one-time activity but as an ongoing commitment.

Security checks and assessments should be continuously updated to address emerging threats and vulnerabilities.

Incident response plans should be in place to handle security incidents that may occur during the deployment process.

Security awareness and training should be provided to all team members to ensure that security is a shared responsibility.

In summary, integrating security into CI/CD pipelines is essential for modern software development.

It enables organizations to deliver software quickly and securely by automating security checks, codifying security policies, and implementing security gates.

By shifting security left in the development process, organizations can identify and remediate vulnerabilities early, reducing the risk of security breaches in production environments.

**Conclusion**

In the UNIX and Linux System Administration Handbook bundle, we have embarked on a comprehensive journey through the multifaceted world of system administration, spanning various critical domains. In Book 1, "UNIX and Linux System Administration Handbook: Networking and Security Essentials," we delved into the core principles of networking and security, establishing a strong foundation for system administrators.

Moving forward, in Book 2, "UNIX and Linux System Administration Handbook: Cloud Integration and Infrastructure as Code," we explored the dynamic realm of cloud computing and the principles of Infrastructure as Code (IaC). This not only allowed us to harness the power of cloud platforms but also provided insights into managing infrastructure with code, ensuring scalability and efficiency.

Book 3, "UNIX and Linux System Administration Handbook: Performance Tuning and Scaling," enabled us to fine-tune and optimize systems for peak performance. We delved into the intricacies of system metrics, profiling tools, and various tuning strategies, equipping administrators with the knowledge needed to make systems run at their best.

Finally, in Book 4, "UNIX and Linux System Administration Handbook: DevOps and Continuous Integration/Continuous Deployment (CI/CD)," we explored the world of DevOps, emphasizing the importance of automation, collaboration, and a continuous delivery pipeline. By mastering the principles of CI/CD, administrators gained the ability to streamline development processes and deliver software efficiently.

This book bundle has provided a comprehensive and holistic approach to system administration, ensuring that administrators are well-equipped to tackle the challenges and complexities of modern IT environments. From networking essentials to cloud integration, performance optimization, and embracing DevOps practices, we have covered it all.

As we conclude this journey, it's important to emphasize that system administration is a dynamic field, constantly evolving with the ever-changing landscape of technology. The knowledge and skills acquired in this bundle are not just valuable assets but also the stepping stones to staying at the forefront of system administration practices.

Whether you are a seasoned professional looking to expand your expertise or a newcomer seeking a solid foundation, the UNIX and Linux System Administration Handbook bundle has provided you with a wealth of knowledge and practical insights to excel in your role.

It's not merely a handbook; it's a comprehensive guide to mastering the diverse facets of system administration in today's complex IT ecosystem.

Embrace this knowledge, apply it with diligence, and continue to explore and innovate in the world of UNIX and Linux system administration. Your journey has just begun, and the possibilities are limitless.

www.ingramcontent.com/pod-product-compliance
Lightning Source LLC
Chambersburg PA
CBHW071236050326
40690CB00011B/2146